Disputed Questions
in the
Liturgy Today

Disputed Questions
in the
Liturgy Today

John M. Huels

Liturgy Training Publications

Liturgy Training Publications
1800 North Hermitage Avenue
Chicago IL 60622-1101
312/486-7008.

Printed in the United States of America.
ISBN 0-930467-95-7

Contents

Abbreviations

AP	*Actio pastoralis,* instruction of the Congregation for Divine Worship on Masses for special groups, May 15, 1969, AAS 61 (1969) 806-11
AAS	*Acta Apostolicae Sedis,* Rome 1909-
BCL	Bishops' Committee on the Liturgy
CIC	*Codex Iuris Canonici auctoritate Ioannis Pauli PP. II promulgatus,* Libreria Editrice Vaticana, 1983
CLD	*Canon Law Digest,* ed. T. Lincoln Bouscaren and James I. O'Connor. Vols. 1-6, Milwaukee–New York: Bruce Publishing Co., 1934-1969. Vols. 7-10, Chicago: Canon Law Digest, 1975-1986
CLSA	Canon Law Society of America
CLSA Comm	*The Code of Canon Law: A Text and Commentary Commissioned by the Canon Law Society of America,* ed. James A. Coriden, Thomas J. Green and Donald E. Heintschel. New York–Mahwah: Paulist Press, 1985
DOL	*Documents on the Liturgy 1963-1979: Conciliar, Papal and Curial Texts,* Collegeville: The Liturgical Press, 1982
DS	*Enchiridion symbolorum, definitionum et declarationum de rebus fidei et morum,* 36th ed., edited by Henricus Denzinger and Adolfus Schönmetzer, Freiburg im Breisgau: Herder, 1976
EM	*Eucharisticum mysterium,* instruction of the Congregation of Rites on worship of the eucharist, May 25, 1967, AAS 59 (1967) 539-73
GIRM	General Instruction of the Roman Missal
ICEL	International Commission on English in the Liturgy
LFM	Lectionary for Mass, introduction to the second edition (1981) of the *Ordo Lectionum Missae*
NCCB	National Conference of Catholic Bishops
PCS	Pastoral Care of the Sick: Rites of Anointing and Viaticum
RCIA	Rite of Christian Initiation of Adults
SC	*Sacrosanctum Concilium,* Constitution on the Liturgy of Vatican II, December 4, 1963, AAS 56 (1964) 97-138
USCC	United States Catholic Conference

Introduction

The words *quaestiones disputatae* may suggest scholastic debates on abstract concepts in philosophy and theology, but the disputed questions of this book are canonical and liturgical issues that, to a greater or lesser extent, are sources of current controversy in the Roman Catholic church. Some of these disputed issues have been sources of tension between ecclesiastical authorities and scholars, ministers and other persons and groups in local churches. Some of the questions find scholars in support of the hierarchy against certain practices in need of reform. On every issue disagreement exists at some level, especially that of praxis.

The principal aim of most of the essays in this book is to see what light canon law can shed on the disputed issues. At times canon law provides straightforward answers to resolve disputes, but often it does not. Rarely can one settle complex issues involving fields such as sacramental theology, liturgical studies, canon law and the pastoral ministry solely by reference to the narrow, literal wording of the directives in the liturgical books and the canons in the Code of Canon Law. Rather, the law must always be interpreted in its historical and theological, as well as legal, context. Nor can the interpreter of the law neglect to be attentive to the experience and wisdom of the people of God, especially in matters touching so vital and central a part of church life as the liturgy.

The essays in this book are not intended merely to repeat what the law says, but rather to interpret the law, to engage in canonical hermeneutics. Those who read these essays are likewise encouraged to become actively involved in this interpretative task. An initial way to do this is to call to consciousness some of the chief presuppositions one has, the influences and viewpoints that affect the ways church, liturgy and indeed all reality are variously perceived. Below are listed seven fundamental principles found in the Code of Canon Law, all of which are based on texts of Vatican II or long-standing tradition. These principles have greatly influenced the way I as a canonist interpret the church's law. I invite my readers to ask themselves to what extent these seven principles are fundamental to the way that they view the church and its liturgy and laws.

Basic Principles

1. **In virtue of their baptism, all the faithful enjoy a true equality and dignity.** (Cf. canon 208.) All the members of Christ's body—male or female, adult or child, cleric, religious or lay—all share a fundamental equality in the church in virtue of their rebirth in Christ through baptism. This implies that whenever a canonical, liturgical or other question is disputed, that interpretation should be preferred which best fosters the equality and dignity of persons in accord with their own condition and function in the church.

2. **The faithful have a right to receive from ordained ministers the spiritual goods of the church, especially the word of God and the sacraments.** (Cf. canon 213.) The faithful have a fundamental right to be nourished by God's word and the sacraments.

Whenever there is a doubt about the interpretation of a law regulating the liturgy, that interpretation must be favored which allows access by the faithful to God's word and the sacraments.

3. **The faithful, conscious of their own responsibility, are bound by Christian obedience to follow what the leaders of the church legislate.** (Cf. canon 212, §1.) A chief purpose of law in any society is to maintain harmony in the community. Since this is also true of the church, it is necessary that laws be respected and obeyed lest division arise in Christ's body. When a dispute arises in the community over a question of liturgical discipline, and the meaning of the law is clear, recourse to the law should settle the dispute. However, when the meaning of a liturgical law itself is in dispute, that interpretation should be favored which best fosters the deepest purpose of the law, namely, the harmonious ordering of the living, worshiping community.

4. **Everyone should avoid proposing their own opinions as the teaching of the church on questions that are open to various opinions.** (Cf. canon 227.) There is a temptation to treat the law as an easy answer to every problem and in the process to oversimplify the church's position. The church is the whole people of God, with a long and still developing history that has seen divergent practices and viewpoints. Often this richness cannot be captured by a resort to a literal reading of one law in isolation from other sources and contextual information.

5. **Liturgical actions are not private but are celebrations of the church itself.** (Cf. canon 837.) The liturgy is not solely the prerogative of the presider, stipend donor, other individual or small group, but is the action of the church. Whenever an issue of liturgy or law is in question, that interpretation must be favored which fosters the communal celebration of the liturgy (including penance and anointing) with the presence and active participation of the faithful.

6. **Custom is the best interpreter of laws.** (Cf. canon 27.) This is an ancient axiom in canon law, derived from Roman law. It means that the living practices of the community are the best indicator of the way written laws are to be understood and observed. Of course, local practices contrary to the law are often not good interpretations but may be the result of negligence or abuse.

Nevertheless, the canonical tradition is confident that in many matters the accepted practices of dioceses, parishes and religious communities can be crucial, indeed, the most important factor in deciding how to interpret and observe liturgical laws.

7. **The salus animarum—the salvation of souls—is the supreme law of the church.** (Cf. canon 1752.) This traditional principle is found in the final canon of the code, a most fitting way to conclude a book of church laws. It means that the spiritual good of the faithful is the highest law, and therefore this primary value must never be neglected when interpreting ecclesiastical law.

Contents

Of the 11 essays in this book, ten have appeared as articles in *Liturgy 80, Catechumenate, Worship* and *Emmanuel.* The many favorable comments on these articles prompted me to accept an invitation to revise and update the essays and gather them into a collection more readily accessible to lay and ordained ministers, liturgists, canonists, students and others interested in current canonical and pastoral issues pertaining to the liturgy of the Latin rite Catholic church. Given the broad audience intended for this work, I have attempted to limit the number of footnotes and restrict them for the most part to studies in the English language. The following notes will introduce each of the essays.

1. **Age for confirmation.** The first essay treats a highly disputed question in the church today. General consensus exists among scholars that the three sacraments of initiation are most fittingly celebrated in a single rite, as in the RCIA, but the law of the Latin church requires that the confirmation and first communion of persons baptized as infants be delayed until they reach the age of reason. In light of this discipline—as well as historical, theological and pastoral considerations— confirmation is optimally conferred on children at about the age of seven during the eucharist at which they also receive their first communion.

2. **Lay preaching.** The second essay examines the church's law on preaching by lay persons in view of the 1983 code and a 1987

decision of the Pontifical Commission for the Authentic Interpretation of the Code of Canon Law, which ruled that the bishop may not dispense from the law that restricts the homily at liturgy to a cleric. By examining the legal meaning of "homily," one discovers that canon law is open to lay preaching in many situations, even in some cases during the liturgy.

3. **Female altar servers.** The question treated in the third essay is one debated among canonists—the legality of female altar servers at eucharist. This is canonically the most technical essay in the book, but it is included because at the present time this disputed question has practical importance in many parishes. There are good legal arguments both opposed to and in favor of the lawfulness of the ministry of server being exercised by women or girls. It appears that a doubt of law exists, and one can therefore conclude that this ministry need not be restricted to males. Even if the law on women exercising liturgical ministries is revised soon in response to the petitions of many bishops, this essay can still serve as a useful exercise in canonical interpretation.

4. **Concelebration.** Eucharistic concelebration is frequently a source of tension in the life of the church today between those who favor and those who oppose it as a regular practice. The fourth essay suggests that a proper understanding of both the relevant canon law, as well as an appreciation of the diverse mentalities of those with strong views on this issue, can help to ease some of this tension so that the eucharist remains the celebration par excellence of church unity.

5. **Mass intentions.** The subject of the fifth essay is the publicity of Mass intentions, that is, the prayer intentions of donors who have given monetary offerings (stipends) to priests to "apply" Masses for those intentions. Scholars have pointed out numerous theological problems posed by the Mass offering system. However, because of financial and other reasons, it is unlikely that the practice will easily disappear. As a result, it is important to avoid publicizing Mass intentions in such a way as to distort their significance by giving them undue emphasis in the eucharistic celebration.

6. **Reducing the number of Masses.** Diocesan bishops in increasing numbers have been calling for a reduction of the number of Sunday Masses in parishes principally in order to improve the overall quality of participation by eliminating sparsely attended celebrations. However, many pastors have not complied with the universal law and diocesan policies on this issue. Based chiefly on relevant texts of canon law and other documentation from the Apostolic See, the sixth essay looks at important liturgical and pastoral considerations for eliminating unnecessary Masses.

7. **First confession.** The seventh essay appears here for the first time in print. It treats the pastoral and canonical questions surrounding the disputed issue of whether the first confession of children should precede or follow their first communion. While many pastors, parents and religious educators prefer that children make their first confession a year or two after their first communion, this practice is not favored by the Apostolic See. Nevertheless, when the law is carefully examined, one finds that children who are properly disposed for first communion should not be denied the sacrament merely because they have not made their first confession.

8. **General absolution.** An intensely disputed question in the church today is the lawfulness and desirability of celebrating in some situations the sacrament of penance with general confession and absolution. The eighth essay is a commentary on the relevant canon law on general absolution. It shows that general absolution may only be used in limited circumstances, but also that these circumstances can exist at times even in regions where there is no shortage of priests.

9. **Who may be anointed.** The spread of communal celebrations of the anointing of the sick has given rise in some places to the abuse of administering the sacrament to those who are ineligible, particularly to those who are not seriously ill. The ninth essay treats the standard requirements for receiving the anointing of the sick and special cases, such as alcoholics, young children and mentally handicapped persons. Although this issue is not disputed by scholars, the existence of seemingly widespread abuses suggests that many ministers and recipients

of anointing may be dissenting in practice from the meaning and scope of this sacrament as envisioned in canon law and the liturgical rite.

10. **Mixed marriages and eucharist.** Should a mixed marriage be celebrated during the eucharist? This question is addressed in the tenth essay. There are good reasons for celebrating the eucharist in some circumstances at the marriage of two parties, one of whom is Catholic and the other a member of another Christian denomination. In general, however, important theological, ecumenical, canonical and other considerations militate against the practice of celebrating mixed marriages during the eucharist.

11. **Concerts in churches.** The final essay is a commentary on a letter of the Congregation for Divine Worship dealing with concerts in churches. The letter was issued largely in response to a dispute in Italy, but its ostensibly restrictive provisions were greeted with great dismay by liturgical musicians and other concerned persons in the United States and elsewhere. An examination of the juridical nature and weight of the document and its contents, considered in light of other relevant laws, reveals that the Apostolic See does not intend to bar concerts in churches, but instead is highly supportive of pastoral musicians and good music, especially sacred and religious music.

These eleven essays cover diverse topics united by the theme of "disputed questions" of liturgical law and praxis. Their order is suggested by the traditional ordering of the sacraments, with the last essay treating an issue of liturgical law that is only in some respects concerned with liturgical celebrations. Since they are discrete topics, however, they can be read in any order desired.

This book is dedicated to my teachers at the Catholic University of America where I studied canon law from 1979 to 1982, especially those professors whose scholarship is related to the topics of this book: Frederick McManus, Ladislas Orsy, SJ, R. Kevin Seasoltz, OSB, Thomas Green and James Provost.

John M. Huels, OSM, JCD
Catholic Theological Union

Age for Confirmation

Few pastoral-liturgical questions in recent years have occasioned greater difference of opinion among segments of Latin rite Catholics than has the issue of the age for confirmation. Since the revised Rite of Confirmation was promulgated in 1971, and even before that in some places, the trend has been to delay confirmation beyond the canonical age of seven. The rationale for this delay is the theological position that holds that confirmation is a "sacrament of spiritual maturity" whose recipients must be able to make a mature commitment to the faith of their baptism, which they received as infants. As a result, the age for confirmation in the United States now varies from diocese to diocese and within some dioceses from parish to parish. The actual age often seems quite arbitrarily chosen on the basis of what someone in authority believes to be the age when a mature commitment is possible.

Despite the prevailing trend toward a higher age for confirmation, in more recent years religious educators and pastoral ministers in increasing numbers have been persuaded to adopt a quite different view of confirmation. The scholarship of liturgists and others has demonstrated to them that the significance of this second sacrament of Christian life is best disclosed when it is celebrated together with baptism and eucharist, the other sacraments of initiation. Hence, an effort is being made in some parishes and dioceses to try to restore the original, proper and authentic sequence of Christian initiation by celebrating confirmation immediately after baptism or, in the case of those baptized as infants, immediately before the reception of first communion.

Richard P. Moudry, for example, has described the pastoral and theological values behind the practice in his parish of celebrating confirmation and first communion at the same celebration in the presence of the bishop.[1] Among the advantages Moudry lists for this practice is that it is "canonically feasible," which is certainly true, albeit an understatement. Indeed, it would not be an exaggeration to say that the policy for children's initiation in Moudry's parish is the normative practice prescribed or, at least, preferred in canon law.

This essay will consider several reasons why experts today by and large favor an earlier, rather than a later, age for the confirmation of those who were baptized as infants. Relevant laws from the Code of Canon Law and the liturgical books will be cited to establish what is legally permissible and desirable regarding the age for confirmation in the Latin church. To contextualize this treatment there will first be a brief overview of some aspects of the complex history of confirmation. This will bring out the sacrament's ritual and theological relatedness to baptism and eucharist.[2] A few remarks will also be made on the minister of confirmation in relation to this discussion.

Historical-Theological Context

According to the common consensus of scholars today, the early tradition of the church does not witness to a separate rite of confirmation apart from baptism, but rather points to a unified initiation rite that included the elements of washing with water, the imposition of hands (in some traditions), anointing with oil and the completion of initiation with full participation in the eucharist. Infants who were baptized were also confirmed and received communion; indeed, infant communion did not die out in the West until about 1200 and it is still practiced in Eastern churches.

In the early centuries the postbaptismal anointing with the oil blessed by the bishop was so much an integral part of the initiation ritual that it was not perceived to be a separate sacrament. The initiation liturgies in most areas contained only one postbaptismal anointing, which was administered either by the bishop or a presbyter. This is still the practice in Eastern churches today, as it also is in the Latin church at the initiation of those seven and older according to the Rite of Christian Initiation of Adults.

The original minister of all the sacraments was the bishop, but as the church began to grow and dioceses spread out to the rural areas, it became impossible for the bishop to preside everywhere and so the presbyters also began to celebrate the sacraments. In most places presbyters performed the full rite of initiation, including the postbaptismal rituals which later came to be called confirmation.

An exception was the initiatory pattern of the diocese of Rome and neighboring areas that followed the Roman practice. There the imposition of hands and anointing on the forehead were reserved to the bishop and so had to be delayed when baptism was administered by a presbyter or deacon until it was possible for the bishop to be present. This Roman pattern of splitting the initiation rite into separate rites performed by separate ministers became predominant in the Western church after the Carolingian reforms of the eighth and ninth centuries. Liturgists refer to this medieval development as a "disintegration" or "degeneration" of sacramental initiation.

As a result of studies uncovering the history of confirmation, contemporary theologians have been critical of the above-mentioned "spiritual maturity" theology and praxis of confirmation. They argue not only that it does not correspond to the origins of the sacrament, but also that it ritually and theologically demands too much of confirmation to the diminishment of baptism and eucharist.

Baptism is the principal sacrament of faith in which believers receive the gift of the Holy Spirit. The other major sacrament of Christian life, the eucharist, is the sacrament that completes initiation into the church. When confirmation is delayed until after the reception of the eucharist, the sequence of initiation is disrupted and it appears that confirmation, rather than eucharist, completes initiation. When greater maturity in the recipients is required for confirmation than for first communion, the significance of confirmation is maximized to the diminution of the eucharist. The appearance of a diminishment of baptism and eucharist in relation to confirmation also results from the practice of reserving confirmation for a higher-ranking minister, namely the bishop, than is typical for the celebration of baptism and first eucharist.

Canonical Discipline

The age prescribed in canon law for the confirmation of those baptized as infants is "about the age of discretion," that is, about seven years of age, also called the age of reason (canon 891). The Rite of Confirmation, n. 11, states that confirmation is "postponed" until this age, which recalls the original practice of confirming immediately after baptism. If someone is in danger of death or when there is some other grave cause in the judgment of the minister, confirmation can be administered at another age, even to infants right after baptism. An infant in canon law is anyone under seven or anyone who lacks the use of reason.

Canon law does not require that those to be confirmed have the use of reason. The code says, rather, that "if they have the use of reason, they must be suitably instructed, properly disposed, and able to renew their baptismal promises" (canon 889, §2). In the case of first communion, however, the use of reason is required, as well as "sufficient knowledge and careful preparation."[3] Thus, more knowledge and preparation are required in canon law of those receiving first communion than of those being confirmed.

A general exception to the age of seven is permitted for a region when its episcopal conference determines another age for confirmation (canon 891). According to this provision, it is possible that the age chosen by the bishops might be either earlier or later than seven. However, when canon 891 is read together with the Rite of Confirmation, n. 11, it is more likely that the legislator has in mind "a more mature age after appropriate formation."

The National Conference of Catholic Bishops (NCCB) of the United States voted in 1972 and again in 1984 to permit each diocesan bishop to determine the age for confirmation in his own diocese. A literal reading of this policy would enable a bishop to establish any age, not excluding the possibility of confirming infants immediately after baptism. However, the intent of the NCCB decision is to conform to the Latin rite discipline. Thus, the policy is best interpreted to mean that the age for confirmation in the United States is the age of reason or at an older age when permitted by diocesan law. In the absence of diocesan legislation, the sacrament must be conferred about the age of discretion as required by universal law, unless there is danger of death or some other grave reason for confirming at a younger age in the judgment of the minister.

For those baptized according to the RCIA, namely, those who are seven years old or older and have the use of reason, all three sacraments of initiation *must* be given at the same celebration.[4] When those seven or older with the use of reason are baptized, their confirmation can be delayed only for a grave reason, for example, in danger of death when the minister who baptizes is not a priest or, even when he is a priest, if he lacks the sacred chrism. It is contrary to the law to postpone the confirmation of children who are of catechetical age when they are baptized simply because they have not reached the age of other confirmandi in the parish. This abuse also offends against good theology and deprives these children of a sacrament that they have a legal right to receive.

What is the best age for the confirmation of children baptized as infants, given the history of confirmation, its ritual and theological relation to baptism and eucharist and the canonical discipline of the Latin church? When the relevant laws are viewed in light of the history and theology of the sacrament, it becomes evident that confirmation ought to be administered at the same celebration in which children of about seven make their first communion.[5] This is most clearly seen in the Rite of

Confirmation, 13, which states that Christian initiation "reaches its culmination in the communion of the body and blood of Christ. The newly confirmed *should therefore participate in the eucharist which completes their Christian initiation.'*[6] This law says that the newly confirmed *should* make first communion in the same ceremony, not *must*.[7] While it admits of exceptions, the law establishes what ought to be the normative practice.

The promotion of the cause of unity between the Catholic and Orthodox churches is another important reason for returning to the original and proper sequence of sacramental initiation. The official Orthodox-Catholic dialogue commission, established by Pope John Paul II and Ecumenical Patriarch Dimitrios I, issued a statement in 1987 that criticizes the practice "in certain Latin churches" of inverting the traditional order of the sacraments of initiation. The statement says: "This inversion, which provokes objections or understandable reservations both by Orthodox and Roman Catholics, calls for deep theological and pastoral reflection because pastoral practice should never lose sight of the meaning of the early tradition and its doctrinal importance." The joint statement also notes that "the disciplinary directives which called for the traditional order of the sacraments of Christian initiation have never been abrogated."[8]

Minister of Confirmation

The original value behind the delay of confirmation seems to have been to allow the bishop, when he could not be present to baptize, at least to be able to perform the imposition of hands and anointing so that he could have some part in the initiation of each person in his diocese. This traditional value of the Western church can continue to be maintained by having the bishop come to parishes for confirmation when it is celebrated together with first communion. In this way the proper sequence of initiation is maintained, the eucharist is seen to be completing initiation, and the bishop's presence at confirmation, a lesser sacrament, does not appear to diminish the principal sacrament of the eucharist.

When the bishop presides at an important sacramental event in the life of the parish, it can be an effective reminder of his role as chief shepherd and principal liturgical celebrant in the whole local church. In large dioceses where the bishop cannot celebrate all the confirmations, it seems fitting for him to delegate the pastor to confirm, because the pastor has been entrusted with the pastoral care of the parish and is its recognized leader. Since the pastor typically presides at first communion, it follows that he also ought to preside at confirmation when it is celebrated with first eucharist and the diocesan bishop cannot be there.

On the other hand, the presence of a minister from outside the parish, whether an auxiliary bishop or a delegated priest, can add more solemnity to the celebration of confirmation and first communion. This will also remind the parish that it is part of a larger church.

Conclusion

Many experts on Christian initiation today, including those in the fields of theology and pastoral care, would welcome the restoration in the Western churches of the ancient practice of fully initiating all persons, even infants, with confirmation and eucharist following baptism.[9] Given the present canonical discipline of the Latin rite, however, this is not possible at infant baptism. Therefore, the celebration of confirmation and first eucharist together at the age of about seven, which is normative in canon law, is the best way of maintaining important theological and ritual values concerning confirmation's proper meaning and role within Christian initiation.

Notes

[1]"The Initiation of Children: The Path One Parish Took," *Catechumenate* 9 (July 1987) 27-33.

[2]Some accessible liturgical studies on confirmation include Gerald Austin, *Anointing with the Spirit: The Rite of Confirmation; The Use of Oil and Chrism* (New York: Pueblo, 1985); Frank C. Quinn, "Confirmation Reconsidered: Rite and Meaning," *Worship* 59 (1985) 354-70; Aidan Kavanagh, "Confirmation: A Suggestion from Structure," *Worship* 58 (1984) 386-95; Gabriele Winkler, "Confirmation or Chrismation? A Study in Comparative Liturgy," *Worship* 58 (1984) 2-17; and various authors in *Assembly* 14 (1987) 377-84.

[3]See canons 913-914. This general rule does not prohibit the administration of the eucharist to mentally retarded and other developmentally disabled persons. On this issue see John Huels, *One Table, Many Laws: Essays on Catholic Eucharistic Practice* (Collegeville: Liturgical Press, 1986), chapter 4.

[4]See canon 885; RCIA, 34 (n. 208 in the 1988 text mandated for use in the United States).

[5]Michael J. Balhoff reaches this same conclusion in a thoroughly researched study based on his doctoral dissertation. See "Age for Confirmation: Canonical Evidence," *The Jurist* 45 (1985) 549-87.

[6]Emphasis mine.

[7]For an explanation of verbs of obligation in canon law and its other literary forms, see John Huels, *Liturgical Law: An Introduction* (Washington, DC: Pastoral Press, 1987) 8-18.

[8]See Joint International Commission for Theological Dialogue Between the Roman Catholic Church and the Orthodox Church, joint statement, Faith, Sacraments and the Unity of the Church, 51, August 1, 1987, *Origins* 17 (1988) 743-49.

[9]See, e.g., the studies from various disciplines in Mark Searle, ed., *Alternative Futures For Worship,* vol. 2: *Baptism and Confirmation* (Collegeville: Liturgical Press, 1987).

Lay Preaching

The Pontifical Commission for the Authentic Interpretation of the Code of Canon Law ruled that diocesan bishops could not dispense from canon 767, §1 that reserves the homily at liturgy to a priest or deacon.[1] In other words, the bishop may not dispense from the law to permit those who are not ordained Roman Catholics to give the homily at liturgy. Although this action by the Holy See at first sight may appear wholly to exclude preaching by lay people at liturgical celebrations, this conclusion is unwarranted when the authentic interpretation is seen in light of other canonical norms.

The theological foundation for preaching by lay people is derived from Vatican II, and this teaching is the source for the discipline of the Code of Canon Law. Canon 225, §1, which is based on *Lumen gentium* 33 and *Ad gentes* 21, states the fundamental right and duty of the laity to evangelize, to see that the divine message of salvation is known and accepted by all persons throughout the world.

Canon 759, also based on Vatican II teaching,[2] says that the laity can be called upon to cooperate with the bishop and presbyters in the exercise of the ministry of the word. The ministry of the word consists of various means of evangelization, among which preaching and catechetical formation are primary (canon 761).

Preaching in Churches

Canon 766 directly treats preaching by lay people. Reversing the position taken in the former Code of 1917 (canon 1342, §2), which prohibited lay preaching in churches, this canon of the 1983 code states that "Lay persons *can be admitted to preach* in a church or oratory. . . ." Two conditions are placed on preaching by lay people: (1) It may be done if it is necessary in certain circumstances or if it is useful in particular cases; and (2) lay persons may not give the homily at liturgy, which, according to canon 767, §1, is restricted to the clergy. Canon 766 also provides for the possibility of national legislation on lay preaching enacted by the conference of bishops.

As in the former law, there are no restrictions on preaching by laity outside churches and oratories. Thus, they have complete liberty to preach in homes, meeting halls, on street corners and at other places provided it is not during the liturgy. If a lay person is to preach in a church or oratory, it must be a case of necessity or usefulness.

Cases of necessity would include areas with a shortage of clergy when a priest is unable to celebrate the eucharist or when a priest or deacon is available but is morally impeded from preaching, for example, when he does not speak the language of the congregation. *Cases of usefulness* do not necessarily imply that clergy are unavailable or morally impeded from preaching. Such cases are potentially numerous. Lay people are increasingly being hired as pastoral associates in parishes, as youth and campus ministers, chaplains in hospitals and other full-time pastoral positions, and they are being called upon to preach at liturgies of the word, communion services, celebrations of the liturgy of the hours and so forth. Sometimes one or more lay persons are part of a team that gives parish missions or directs retreats, and preaching is a regular part of their ministry.[3]

It is commonplace in many areas for lay religious or lay missionaries to preach on their apostolates, especially in connection with an annual mission collection. Lay theologians and other qualified and competent lay persons are also occasionally, or even regularly, invited to preach in some churches. Surely, as more and more lay people receive degrees in theology and ministerial studies, the usefulness of preaching by such qualified and dedicated Christians will be more widely recognized and appreciated.

Granting the Permission

Canon 766 implies that the conference of bishops will enact legislation on lay preaching, which presumably will provide a regulation on who is the competent authority to grant the faculty for a lay person to preach in a church or oratory.[4] In the absence of legislation from the episcopal conference, it is the competence of the diocesan bishop to regulate lay preaching in the churches and oratories of his diocese. The bishop has general authority over the liturgy in the diocese and can enact laws and establish local policies, provided they are not contrary to universal law (canons 835, §1; 838, §§1,4; 392). With particular reference to preaching, canon 772, §1 states that "the norms issued by the diocesan bishop concerning the exercise of preaching are to be observed by all."

Can lay people preach in accord with canon 766 when there is neither legislation from the episcopal conference nor a local diocesan policy? It seems the answer should be affirmative. The law implies that it is desirable to have a uniform policy established by the episcopal conference, but where none exists, and where the diocesan bishop has not exercised his authority in this matter, it falls to those in charge of churches or oratories to permit lay preaching when they determine that it is necessary or useful. This is in keeping with the nature of the canonical authority granted to pastors, rectors of churches and religious superiors.[5]

Not the Homily

A second restriction on preaching by lay people is that they cannot give the homily at liturgy. Canon 767, §1 states: "Among the forms of preaching the homily is preeminent; it is a part of the liturgy itself and is reserved to a priest or deacon; in the homily the mysteries of faith and the norms of Christian living are to be expounded from the sacred text throughout the course of the liturgical year."

The canonical legislator strongly recommends that a homily be given whenever a sufficient number of people are present, including weekdays, especially during Advent or Lent or on the occasion of some feast day or time of mourning. On Sundays and holy days of obligation, there is a legal obligation to give a homily whenever a congregation is present, and it cannot be omitted without a serious reason (canon 767, §§2,3).

Canon law considers preaching by priests and deacons to be an important function of their ministry. Ordained ministers, according to canon 762, "are to value greatly the task of preaching since among their principal duties is the proclaiming of the gospel of God to all." The homily is a unique form of preaching at liturgy that brings out the close relationship between the word of God and the mystery of the eucharist. Christ's paschal mystery is proclaimed through the readings and the homily; and it becomes present through the sacrifice of the Mass.[6]

According to liturgical law, the homily of the Mass is ordinarily given by the one presiding.[7] By exception, it can be given by a concelebrant or the deacon or some other priest. If the homily is given by someone other than the presider, it is highly desirable that he participate in the entire eucharist. According to the NCCB Committee on Life and Ministry, "The practice of having a preacher slip in to read the Gospel and preach the homily, and then slip out again, does not do justice to the liturgical integrity of the homily."[8]

The homily is based on one or more of the scripture readings proclaimed at the Mass and/or some other text of the liturgy being celebrated that day, and should be accommodated to the needs of the listeners (GIRM, 41). An important goal of the homily is to lead the gathered community to a fruitful celebration of the eucharist (LFM, 24).

As a result of the laws and principles cited in the foregoing paragraphs, it becomes evident why lay persons are prohibited from preaching the homily at Mass. Not only is preaching a principal duty of ordained ministers, but the homily is a special kind of preaching that is intended to bring together the liturgy of the word and the liturgy of the eucharist. As such, it is a liturgical function best fulfilled by the priest who presides at both liturgy of the word and liturgy of the eucharist.

Lay Preaching at Liturgy

Does this mean that the laity may never preach at Mass or another liturgical celebration? This is not a necessary conclusion. They may not give the homily, but they are not excluded from preaching altogether. The homily is one form of preaching, not the only form. According to the clear wording of canon 767, §1, a homily is (1) a form of preaching, which is (2) part of the liturgy itself, and which is (3) reserved to a priest or deacon. Whenever a lay person preaches, whether during Mass or at some other time, they cannot be giving a homily since only clergy—by definition—can give a homily. Another way of putting it is to say that a homily is like a presidential address: Only the president can deliver the presidential address.[9]

This nominalistic interpretation of the canonical meaning of the homily, proposed by James Provost in 1983,[10] appears to be confirmed by the 1987 authentic interpretation of the Pontifical Commission for the Authentic Interpretation of the Code of Canon Law. Although the pontifical commission did not give a reason for its decision prohibiting bishops from dispensing from canon 767, §1, Cardinal Rosalio Castillo Lara, the president of the commission, indicated that he believes canon 767, §1 is a constitutive law.[11]

A constitutive law treats a matter that is essential and fundamental and therefore such laws may not be dispensed (canon 86). In reference to the homily this means, then, that of its very essence the homily is a form of preaching reserved to ordained ministers. To say that the bishop cannot dispense from canon 767, §1 is only to say that the bishop cannot change the definition of what a homily is. It does not mean that permission could not be granted for a lay person to exercise some other form of preaching at Mass.

Further confirmation of this view can be seen in two documents of the Holy See, the 1973 Directory for Masses with Children and the 1988 Directory for Sunday Celebrations in the Absence of a Presbyter.[12] The 1973 directory allows an adult lay person, with the consent of the pastor or rector of the church, to speak at a Mass for children after the gospel, especially if the priest finds it difficult to adapt himself to the mentality of children. The directory does not say that the lay person can give a homily, which is restricted by law to the clergy. The lay person truly can preach the word of God to the children, but it is a form of preaching that cannot be called a homily because it is not being done by a Catholic cleric.

The 1988 Directory for Sunday Celebrations in the Absence of a Presbyter gives general principles for Sunday liturgical services when a priest cannot be present to preside at Mass. After the readings from the scriptures of the day, the directory permits a lay presider to give an "explanation of the readings," or there may be a period of meditative silence. As another option, the directory states that a homily prepared by the absent pastor might be read by the lay presider. Clearly, this bears out the nominalistic definition of a homily as that form of preaching at liturgy that is restricted to a cleric. When a lay person reads a homily, he or she is reading it on behalf of the pastor or other authorized cleric who wrote it, and thus it is the pastor's words, not the lay person's, which make it a homily. Lay persons can truly preach, as explicitly provided for in canon 766, but when lay people preach in their own words it is a form of preaching that cannot be called a homily. It must be called something else, such as an "explanation of the readings" or perhaps a "sermon," a "reflection on the word" or some other term.

A homily is a form of preaching at liturgy, delivered by a cleric or at least read in the name of an authorized cleric. If one examines the law closely, it is clear that the word "preaching" is generic; "homily" is only one species of the genus "preaching." When a cleric preaches at liturgy, it is a homily. When a cleric preaches outside the liturgy, or when a lay person preaches, it cannot be called a homily because it does not fit the definition implied in the law. On the other hand, when a lay person reads a homily prepared by the pastor or another authorized cleric at liturgy, it is truly a homily because its authorship is avowedly clerical and the setting is officially liturgical.[13]

In this understanding of the meaning of homily, lay preaching can at times be lawful even at the eucharistic liturgy. The following would be examples of when lay persons might licitly preach during the eucharist (keeping in mind that a homily by a priest or deacon is required on Sundays and holy days unless there is a serious reason for omitting it):

1. A lay person could preach on weekdays when a homily by a priest or deacon is not required by law. Although canon law favors the liturgical homily on weekdays given by the presider, if the presider or another cleric does not give the homily, another form of preaching by a lay person would be possible within the limits of the law.

2. A lay person could preach in addition to the homily of the priest or deacon on Sundays and holy days of obligation. A common example is the case of certain kinds of special appeals, such as mission collections in which the presider first gives a brief homily before the lay person preaches. In this case the homily is not omitted; another form of preaching is simply added for an important reason or on a special occasion.

3. The competent authority could permit a lay person to preach in place of the homily on Sundays and holy days of obligation if there were a serious reason for omitting the homily. A 1973 letter of the Congregation for the Clergy, in an indult permitting lay preaching in Germany, mentioned two cases when a lay person could preach at Mass in place of the homily:

(a) when the presider is physically or morally impeded from giving the homily and no other priest or deacon is available;

(b) by reason of special circumstances, for example, on a feast for the safeguarding of Christian family life, for the fostering of works of charity, for the promotion of missions among the nations and on other feasts according to the decision of the bishop.[14]

The latter case implies that on certain special occasions the pastoral benefit to be derived from allowing a competent lay person to preach for a particular purpose is itself a sufficiently serious reason to omit the homily by the presider or other cleric.

Qualifications

Whoever preaches in a church or oratory should be qualified and competent. Universal law presumes that the clergy are qualified to preach due to their formation before ordination. For that reason the law itself grants to all presbyters and deacons the faculty to preach everywhere. This faculty can be exercised with the presumed consent of the rector of the church, unless the faculty was restricted or taken away by competent authority or unless express permission is required by particular law (canon 764).

Lay persons, too, should have appropriate formation if they are to preach in church. They should have sufficient knowledge in the fields of scripture and theology; and they should have preparation for or experience in public speaking. As noted above, lay religious and other lay persons are increasingly attending seminaries and graduate schools of theology and ministry, and are taking the same courses and obtaining the same or similar degrees as those who are going to be ordained.

Not all lay persons who might be called upon to preach will have such clear-cut, certifiable competence. Sometimes a lay person may lack a formal degree, but may be a good communicator, conversant with the scriptures and church teachings, and committed to the apostolate. Because of the difficulty the pastor or superior might experience in deciding at times on who is qualified, it would be desirable to have a uniform policy for lay preaching at the level of the diocese or the episcopal conference.

Canon 213 of the code states the fundamental right of the faithful to receive from ordained ministers the spiritual goods of the church, especially the word of God and the sacraments. With the worsening shortage of clergy in the church today, the ministry of lay persons, including those who are competent to preach, will be increasingly necessary to ensure that all the faithful have adequate opportunity to be nourished by God's holy word.

Notes

[1]Reply, May 26, 1987, *Communicationes* 19 (1987) 261.

[2]For references to pertinent Vatican II documents, see James A. Coriden, "The Teaching Office of the Church," CLSA Comm, 550.

[3]See canon 770.

[4]At the time of this writing, guidelines on lay preaching are in preparation by the NCCB. See *BCL Newsletter* 24 (1988) 16.

[5]See canons 764; 765; 767, §4; 561; and 528, §1.

[6]See SC, 6, 47; and LFM, 10, 24.

[7]GIRM, 42; LFM, 24.

[8]See *Fulfilled in Your Hearing: The Homily in the Sunday Assembly* (Washington DC: USCC, 1982) 23.

[9]See William Skudlarek, "Lay Preaching and the Liturgy," *Worship* 58 (1984) 505.

[10]"Lay Preaching and Canon Law in a Time of Transition," in *Preaching and the Non-Ordained: An Interdisciplinary Study* (Collegeville: Liturgical Press, 1983) 134-58.

[11]Private reply, December 3, 1986, reported in *Roman Replies and CLSA Advisory Opinions* (Washington DC: CLSA, 1987) 6-7.

[12]Congregation for Divine Worship, Directory for Masses with Children, *Pueros baptizatos,* 24, November 1, 1973, AAS 66 (1974) 30-46; DOL, 2157; Congregation for Divine Worship, Directory for Sunday Celebrations in the Absence of a Presbyter, *Christi Ecclesia,* 43, May 22, 1988, prot. n. 691/86.

[13]"Liturgy" is understood here as the celebration of the rites found in the liturgical books approved by competent ecclesiastical authority.

[14]Letter to the German episcopal conference, November 20, 1973, CLD 8:943; DOL, 2958.

Female Altar Servers

At the 1987 Synod of Bishops on the role of the laity, many bishops called for the elimination of restrictions against women functioning in lay liturgical ministries, notably the permanent ministries of acolyte and lector. The American Catholic hierarchy has long supported such a change. Already in 1971 the Bishops' Committee on the Liturgy declared: "It is certain that in the liturgical celebration, as in other facets of the church's life, there should be no discrimination or apparent discrimination against women. . . . The basic or radical equality of the baptized members of Christ takes priority over, and is more significant than, distinctions of order and ministry."[1]

At the time of this writing, there have been no changes in church law on this matter since the revised Code of Canon Law went into effect in 1983. According to the code, only men may be permanently instituted as lectors and acolytes. Women may serve as lectors on a temporary basis, but no mention is made of altar servers or temporary acolytes.

Although no change has yet come about, more and more parishes have been allowing women or girls to serve the priest at Mass instead of only boys or men as in the previous discipline. Has this practice been lawful? May women and girls function as altar servers at the eucharist under the discipline of the revised Code of Canon Law even without a change in law that expressly permits this?

This question has been disputed by canonists. Some claim that the universal law prohibits women and girls from serving the priest at the eucharist, while others assert that the 1983 code has eliminated restrictions against this. Both positions will be sketched here along with a canonical analysis of relevant church documents and their nature, weight and binding force. Whether or not the law changes soon, the arguments presented here may serve as a useful exercise in the science of interpreting canon law.

Arguments against Female Servers

Several legal arguments are proposed by canonists who maintain that women and girls are prohibited by universal law from serving at eucharist. These are based principally on the new code and the liturgical law.

The Revised Code. The Code of Canon Law makes no mention of altar servers. However, it expressly states that only men may be instituted as permanent acolytes (canon 230, §1), a ministry for which the function of server is a substitution or supplement. The permanently instituted lector is the only other lay ministry in the code that is restricted to men. While the law permits women to be deputed as lectors on a temporary basis (canon 230, §2), there is no express provision for women to function temporarily as acolytes.

Canon 230, §2 also states that lay persons, male or female, may be temporarily deputed to function as commentator, cantor, or in other liturgical roles according to the norm of law. Can one not conclude, therefore, that the law prohibits females from serving at the altar? If the legislator intended such a possibility, surely this canon would have been the logical place to express it.

The Liturgical Law. Liturgical law is expressly excluded "for the most part" (canon 2) from the legal concerns treated in the code. Canon 2 says in part that liturgical laws that are in force retain their force unless there is something contrary to them in the canons of the code. There is a whole other body of ecclesiastical law known as liturgical law found principally in the introductions and rubrics of the liturgical books. The liturgical laws retain their force provided that other universal laws enacted later than the liturgical laws are not contrary to them, whether these later laws are found in the code or another source (canons 6, §1, 2°; 20).

Some of those who argue against female altar servers cite statements from two postconciliar liturgical documents, apparently in the belief that they are still in force. The 1970 instruction of the Congregation for Divine Worship, *Liturgicae instaurationes,* states in paragraph one of n. 7: "In conformity with norms traditional in the church, women (single, married, religious), whether in churches, homes, convents, schools or institutions for women, are barred from serving the priest at the altar."[2] The 1980 instruction of the Congregation for Sacraments and Divine Worship, *Inaestimabile donum,* refers to this norm of the 1970 instruction in its footnote to n. 18. *Inaestimabile donum,* 18 states: "There are various roles which a woman may fulfill in the liturgical assembly. Among these are reading from the word of God and proclaiming the intentions at the prayers of the faithful. However, women are not permitted to undertake the functions of acolyte or minister at the altar."[3]

Another relevant text is n. 70 of the General Instruction of the Roman Missal, which states in its first paragraph: "Lay men, even if they have not received institution as ministers, may perform all the functions below those reserved to deacons. At the discretion of the rector of the church, women may be appointed to ministries that are performed outside the sanctuary."[4] According to this norm women may function only in those liturgical roles that are performed outside the sanctuary. This excludes women from serving at eucharist because the function of altar server is exercised within the sanctuary.

Certain laws enacted after 1969, when the GIRM was first promulgated, nevertheless permit women to minister in the sanctuary, as in the case of lectors and special ministers of communion. However, these other laws must be understood as exceptions to the general rule stated in GIRM, 70.[5] Moreover, the principle of canon 21 states: "In a case of doubt the revocation of a preexistent law is not presumed, but later laws are to be related to earlier ones and, insofar as possible, harmonized with them." Canon 21 yields a presumption in favor of the continuing force of GIRM, 70.

Arguments for Female Servers

Three principal arguments support the view that there is no prohibition in the universal law against women or girls serving at the altar: (1) the code does not exclude female altar servers, but states instead that they may exercise liturgical functions without specifying each one in particular; (2) the norms of *Liturgicae instaurationes* and *Inaestimabile donum* that prohibit female servers are no longer in force as a result of the revision of the code; (3) the first paragraph of GIRM, 70 is revoked by the new code or is at least implicitly abrogated due to its obsolescence.

The Revised Code. Canon 813, §1 of the 1917 code required the presence of a server at Mass. The revised code mentions nothing about the server. Canon 906 instead requires that in addition to the presider there be also participating "at least some member of the faithful except for a just and reasonable cause." This could be a server or any other member of the faithful, male or female. The elimination of the requirement of the server in the new law certainly raises the question why women and girls should continue to be barred from exercising such a minor, wholly optional liturgical function.

Canon 813, §2 of the 1917 code expressly prohibited females from serving Mass, but if no male was available, a woman could respond to the priest provided she did not approach the altar. These restrictions are not contained in the revised code. Since the 1917 code is abrogated by the 1983 code, the prohibition against female altar servers has been removed unless liturgical law provides otherwise.

Why has the legislator removed from the code the prohibition against women serving at Mass? A report of the *coetus,* or subcommittee, on the sacraments of the Pontifical Commission for the Revision of the Code of Canon Law may reveal something about the law's intent on this matter. At a meeting of the *coetus* held in 1978 the question was raised whether to maintain the prohibition against women going near the altar during the eucharist as in canon 813, §2 of the 1917 code. The consultors discussed the issue and concluded that this prohibition was "obsolete" because the supreme legislator had already permitted the possibility of women distributing communion, reading the scriptures and leading the prayers of the faithful. Therefore all but one consultor, who abstained, agreed that the revised code should say nothing about this matter.[6]

The discussion was not about servers per se, but it is closely related to the issue. The restriction against women going to the altar to respond to the priest during the eucharist and the restriction against women serving were conjoined in canon 813, §2 of the former code, and both were eliminated in the new code. The reason given by the *coetus* on the sacraments for removing the prohibition against women going to the altar during the eucharist applies also to the issue of women serving. If a woman may distribute communion, proclaim the readings before the gospel and perform other liturgical ministries, is it reasonable that she should be prevented from exercising a lesser function such as altar server? According to the traditional axiom: "She who can do the greater can also do the lesser."

If the prohibition against women going to the altar during the eucharist to respond to the priest is obsolete, is not therefore the prohibition against a woman or girl serving the priest also obsolete? The vote of the *coetus* on the sacraments to remove the prohibition against women approaching the altar during the eucharist may well indicate that the removal of the prohibition against female altar servers was also a conscious and deliberate decision due to the law's obsolescence.

Another indication of the law's intent might be seen in canon 930, §2, which permits any properly instructed lay person to assist a blind or infirm priest who is celebrating the eucharist. The law refers to a lay person of either sex *(laicus),* not as in canon 230, §1, which restricts the permanent ministries of acolyte and lector to lay men *(viri laici)*. Such an assistant to a blind or infirm priest would necessarily perform some or all of the functions of an altar server. If a woman may serve for a blind or infirm priest, why not for one who is well?

One might also argue that female altar servers are implicitly permitted in the revised code in virtue of canon 230, §2, which states that lay persons, male or female, may fulfill the functions of commentator or cantor *or other functions* in accord with the norm of law. Since altar servers are not mentioned in the code, might not this be one of the "other" liturgical functions that laity of both sexes may perform?[7]

It should also be noted that the revised code espouses the equality and dignity of all Christians (canon 208). All lay ministries and functions specified in the 1983 code are open to men and women alike except for the permanent ministries of lector and acolyte, which are requirements for the reception of holy orders. For example, a woman is able to share in the exercise of the power of governance, also called jurisdiction (canon 129, §2); she may serve as judge in a church court (canon 1421, §2); she may serve as the chancellor of a diocese (canon 483, §2). If such important roles are open to women, is it reasonable to maintain that they should be barred from performing the simple tasks involved in serving at the eucharist?

In sum, the 1983 code does not contain the prohibition of the former code against female altar servers, and it seems that the obsolescence of that prohibition may well have been the motive for its elimination. Further, the code permits a lay person of either sex to assist a blind or infirm celebrant of the eucharist, or to be the sole participant at eucharist when a priest celebrates without a congregation. Moreover, canon 230, §2 broadly permits both men and women to engage in liturgical functions, without excluding the ministry of altar server. Hence, in the revised code not only are women not excluded from serving, but they may expressly function at least in some circumstances in ways that altar servers function.

The Nonlegal Nature of an Instruction. The Holy See issues many different kinds of documents, but few are legislative in nature. For example, the familiar papal document called an "apostolic exhortation" has been used by the pope as a vehicle for his reflections on the subject dealt with at a previous Synod of Bishops. The very title of this document indicates that it is merely exhortative; it does not introduce changes in doctrine or discipline. When the pope wishes to change law, he uses other forms of documents, notably the apostolic constitution or the apostolic letter issued *motu proprio*.

Likewise, an instruction *(instructio)* issued by a Roman congregation is not a legislative text. Even under the discipline of the 1917 code it was clear that instructions are not legal in nature but consist rather of explanations or clarifications of the law.[8] Nevertheless, curial instructions sometimes have introduced changes in church discipline; therefore, early in the process of revising the code, the need was expressed for a clear statement of the distinction between truly legal documents and mere administrative ones.[9] This view was upheld by the leadership of the Pontifical Commission for the Revision of the Code of Canon Law prior to its 1981 plenary assembly.[10]

Canon 34 of the 1983 code reflects the concern of the commission by clearly defining and firmly circumscribing the nature and purpose of instructions. Paragraph 3 of this canon says that one of the ways by which the force of an instruction is lost is by the cessation of the law on which it relied. If the law treated by the instruction is no longer in force, then the part of the instruction dealing with that law also lacks all force even in the administrative arena. In this case, canon 813 of the 1917 code is abrogated by the 1983 code, and therefore the prohibition against female altar servers is removed, provided there is no other liturgical law governing the matter. If no such genuine liturgical law exists, the norms of *Liturgicae instaurationes* and *Inaestimabile donum* that prohibit female altar servers are no longer in force.

The Liturgical Law. We have already seen in the previous arguments against female altar servers that there is a relevant liturgical law, namely, n. 70 of the General Instruction of the Roman Missal. The General Instruction *(institutio,* not *instructio)* of the Roman Missal is the principal source of liturgical law for the celebration of the eucharist. The laws of the liturgical books have the same binding force as the laws of the code.

The first paragraph of GIRM, 70 was included in the first edition of the Roman Missal in 1969. Paragraph two was added in 1975. The entire norm reads:

> Lay men, even if they have not received institution as ministers, may perform all the functions below those reserved to deacons. At the discretion of the rector of the church, women may be appointed to ministries that are performed outside the sanctuary.
>
> The conference of bishops may permit qualified women to proclaim the readings before the gospel and to announce the intentions of the general intercessions. The conference may also more precisely designate a suitable place for a woman to proclaim the word of God in the liturgical assembly.

The second paragraph permits women to proclaim the readings before the gospel and to announce the intentions of the general intercessions. Episcopal conferences are free to designate the place for a woman to proclaim the word of God in the assembly, and the sanctuary area is not excluded in this paragraph. Moreover, the explicit prohibition against women reading in the sanctuary, which had been stated in the 1969 edition of GIRM, 66, was eliminated in the 1975 revision. It is a common observation that in virtually every part of the Catholic world women do indeed read from the scriptures at Mass at the lectern in the sanctuary. In the United States, this practice is authorized by the conference of bishops.[11]

Another liturgical ministry which is performed in the sanctuary and which may be exercised by women is that of special minister of the eucharist (canons 230, §2; 910, §2). This is explicitly acknowledged in the 1975 edition of the GIRM, 68: "As for other ministers, some perform different functions inside the sanctuary, others outside. The first kind include those deputed as special ministers of communion and those who carry the missal, the cross, candles, the bread, wine, water and the thurible." This norm defines the ministry of special minister of the eucharist as one which takes place in the sanctuary, and thus the law itself contradicts the restriction against women ministering at the eucharist in the sanctuary.

Still another liturgical function which a woman may perform under the revised code is that of helper for a blind or infirm priest who is celebrating the eucharist (canon 930, §2). If the blind or infirm priest is celebrating in a church or other sacred place, his assistant, whether male or female, would have to be present in the sanctuary to help him as needed.

The reader, leader of the general intercessions, special minister of the eucharist and assistant to a blind or infirm priest may be a man or woman and the functions of each are performed in the sanctuary. Does this fact not suggest that the first paragraph of GIRM, 70 is obsolete, that its binding force has ceased intrinsically? In the canonical tradition a law is said to have ceased without express revocation when it is obsolete or useless or causes harm to the community. Intrinsic cessation of law occurs due to the passage of time or the changing of circumstances. Paragraph one of GIRM, 70 was viable when it first appeared in 1969, but legislation after that date allowing women to minister in the sanctuary contributed to the obsolescence of such an absolute restriction.

One could also argue that GIRM, 70 has been expressly revoked by later law. Canon 230, §2 permits lay persons, male or female, to fulfill the functions of commentator or cantor *or other functions* in the liturgy in accord with the norm of the law. Ludger Müller maintains that these "other functions" include that of Mass server and that this law therefore abrogates any previous restrictions against women serving as altar servers.[12]

Another argument for the express revocation of GIRM, 70 is based on canon 20 of the code. Canon 20 states that a later law abrogates or derogates from a prior law when it expressly decrees it, or when it is directly contrary to it, or when it completely restructures the matter of the prior law. Clearly, legislation enacted after 1969, when the General Instruction was first published, has completely restructured the matter of women ministering in the sanctuary. The first paragraph of GIRM, 70 must therefore be considered abrogated in light of the 1983 code and the principle of canon 20. Consequently, no prohibition exists in the universal law of the Latin rite against female altar servers.

Conclusion

We have seen the chief arguments on the issue of women and girls serving at the eucharist and the different conclusions that they yield. The strongest legal argument against female servers is based on the fact that the first paragraph of n. 70 of the General Instruction of the Roman Missal bars women from exercising liturgical ministries in the sanctuary. According to this view, those cases in which the law permits women to minister in the sanctuary—such as special minister of communion, lector, leader of the prayers of the faithful—are to be considered exceptions to the general rule. In accord with the principle of canon 21, mentioned above, one should not presume that the first paragraph of GIRM, 70 has been revoked, but it should be harmonized with later laws insofar as possible.

The strongest legal arguments in favor of female servers are: (1) that the revised code has dropped the restriction of the former code against women being in the sanctuary during the eucharist and has made the ministry of server optional; (2) that the code permits women as well as men to assist a blind or infirm priest at Mass and permits women and men to exercise various specified and unspecified liturgical functions, not expressly excluding that of altar server; and (3) that the first paragraph of GIRM, 70 has been expressly abrogated by the revised code or that it has been at least intrinsically revoked by legislation enacted after 1969.

It seems we have a doubt of law. Good legal arguments can be marshaled for either position. Therefore, the rule of canon 14 should be invoked: "When there is a doubt of law, the law does not bind." Since doubtful laws are not binding, it is safe to conclude that women or girls may be altar servers under the present discipline of the universal law of the Latin church. Those parishes that have begun the practice are acting lawfully.

It is quite possible that a change in discipline on this issue may be forthcoming. It is also possible that the doubt in the law could be clarified by an authentic interpretation. Or perhaps this may be a case where the legislator will permit the development of local customs. Up to the 16th century, the principal way that liturgical practices changed was not by law but by custom. Even today the canonical system recognizes the legitimacy of local customs, even those that are contrary to the law (canons 5, 23-27). On the issue of Mass servers, it is likely that the local customs of parishes and dioceses will continue to have more practical relevance than any changes in universal law, at least insofar as there are wise and tolerant pastors of the church who are sensitive to the desires and aspirations of their people.

Notes

[1]Statement, Place of Women in the Liturgy, February 14, 1971, in *Thirty Years of Liturgical Renewal: Statements of the Bishops' Committee on the Liturgy*, ed. Frederick R. McManus (Washington, DC: USCC, 1987) 137.

[2]Instruction on the Orderly Carrying Out of the Constitution on the Liturgy, September 5, 1970, AAS 62 (1970) 692-704; DOL, 525.

[3]Norms Concerning the Worship of the Eucharistic Mystery, April 3, 1980, AAS 72 (1980) 338.

[4]DOL, 1460.

[5]See Francisco Javier Urrutia, "De quibusdam quaestionibus ad librum primum Codicis pertinentibus," *Periodica* 74 (1984) 301-04.

[6]*Communicationes* 13 (1981) 242.

[7]For a thorough exposition of this argument, see Ludger Müller, "Gilt das Verbot der Messdienerinnen noch?" *Archiv für katholisches Kirchenrecht* 155 (1986) 126-37.

[8]Benedict XV, *motu proprio, Cum iuris canonici Codicem,* II, September 15, 1917, AAS 9 (1917) 484.

[9]Report of the *coetus de normis generalibus, Communicationes* 3 (1971) 92.

[10]See *Relatio complectens synthesis animadversionum ab em.mis atque exc.mis patribus commissionis ad novissimum schema Codici Iuris Canonici exhibitarum, cum responsionibus a secretaria et consultoribus datis* (Typis Polyglottis Vaticanis, 1981) 27.

[11]Appendix to the GIRM for the Dioceses of the USA, 66c.

[12]See above, note 7.

Concelebration

Vatican II's restoration of concelebration was warmly welcomed in the 1960s by liturgists and others because, unlike private Masses, the gathering of priests together at the same eucharist better signifies the unity of the church and the unity of the presbyterate assembled at the one table of the Lord. Assuredly, a most beneficial result of concelebration has been the elimination of multiple, private Masses that were often simultaneously celebrated by priests at side altars in the same church with only a server assisting. Liturgists in the 1980s, however, have become increasingly critical of concelebration.[1] Some of their objections center on:

1. **Aesthetics.** Liturgy should open up for worshipers an experience of mystery and the sacred while creating a climate of hospitality and community. According to the Bishops' Committee on the Liturgy, "A simple and attractive beauty in everything that is used or done in liturgy is the most effective invitation to this kind of experience."[2] Concelebration, especially with large numbers, often militates against these

values. Sufficient chasubles of the same style are seldom available and, perhaps through no fault of their own, priests must don albs designed as underclothing and stoles in clashing colors and patterns. The placement and direction of the concelebrants can be a challenge for the most inventive and experienced master of ceremonies. All too often they are crowded in the sanctuary or left standing in the pews blocking the view of the people who choose to kneel. Liturgical law states that the concelebrants are to speak their parts *submissa voce,* or "inaudibly" as directed by the Bishops' Committee on the Liturgy,[3] so that the presider can be clearly heard. In reality, the din during the eucharistic prayer frequently overwhelms the most determined presider and best public-address system. Another distraction occurs sometimes during the communion rite when the distribution of the bread and cup to many concelebrants creates a tedious void in the liturgical action as the assembly passively awaits its turn to receive.

2. **Distorted symbolism.** The theological value of concelebration is primarily its symbolism of the unity of the church and of the eucharistic assembly and secondarily of the unity of the presbyterate. For growing numbers of Catholics, however, concelebration is experienced as a sign and source of disunity and fragmentation in the church. This is true particularly at liturgies for certain kinds of groups, such as in seminaries, religious communities composed of clerics and lay brothers, or mixed assemblies of women religious and clergy. The presence of all the ordained males in the sanctuary or other place of prominence and all the lay religious, seminarians and other laity in the nave is a disturbing or even painful reminder to many of separation and inequality. In such circumstances concelebration may be perceived as a sign of ecclesial division rather than unity.

3. **Notion of priesthood.** The ministerial priesthood is increasingly being understood in a functional or relational way that does not require status distinctions based on an ontological difference between clergy and laity. This means that holy orders is viewed as empowering the ordained for certain ministerial functions and establishing a relationship of pastoral and cultic leadership of and service to the Christian community.

From this perspective, the concelebrant's role is superfluous because the functional and leadership roles at eucharist are carried out by the presider, reader, cantor, musicians and other ministers. Those who see little or no functional role for concelebration may even tend to regard it as a manifestation of clerical privilege and status.

As a result of these and other factors, many priests no longer desire to concelebrate, at least not on a regular basis, and some liturgy planners, religious communities and seminaries have discontinued or discouraged concelebration. These decisions, in turn, have sometimes been met with bewilderment and anger in other priests who wish to concelebrate, and the controversy surrounding concelebration becomes a source of disagreement and discord in the Christian community. In order to deal sensitively with this problem, it is important to understand viewpoints on both sides of the issue. Those who prefer concelebration must try to understand the criticisms of liturgists, and those who oppose the regular practice of concelebration should attempt to understand why many priests prefer to concelebrate rather than to participate in the eucharist like other members of the faithful. Having looked at the critique of concelebration, it would be helpful now to indicate some of the principal reasons why many priests like to concelebrate Mass.

1. **Notion of priesthood.** Some priests have a primarily ontological notion of priesthood, and they understand the sacrament of holy orders as having brought about an essential change in their being which sets them apart from other members of the faithful. For them it is necessary always to have a ministerial role as presider or concelebrant to signify this difference in status. Their very self-concept as priest is strongly identified with and affirmed by their distinctive role in the eucharistic celebration. Such a view of the priesthood might be seen in the 1967 instruction of the Congregation of Rites, *Eucharisticum mysterium,* 43, which says that it is fitting for priests "to take part in the eucharist by exercising the order proper to them, that is, by celebrating or concelebrating the Mass and not simply by receiving communion like the laity."

2. **Priestly spirituality.** Some priests prefer to concelebrate or preside rather than participate at Mass like other members of the faithful for reasons of their own personal piety and spirituality. They may express this by saying that they "get more out of the Mass" by concelebrating than by participating like the laity, or that they are better disposed to receive the graces of the eucharist by an active, specifically presbyteral role in the celebration. Their daily offering of the eucharist is frequently the center and climax of their prayer life. This notion of priestly spirituality seems to underlie the exhortations in the Code of Canon Law in which priests are "earnestly invited" (canon 276, §1, 2°) and "strongly recommended" (canon 904) to celebrate or concelebrate the eucharist daily.

3. **Mass offerings.** Another important motive for concelebration is derived from the acceptance of Mass offerings, formerly called stipends. Canon law allows concelebrants to accept a monetary offering from a donor who wants a specific intention applied to the Mass (canon 945), provided it is the only Mass offering they receive that day (canon 951, §2). Diocesan priests with inadequate income and religious priests who are expected to contribute offerings to their communities may view the daily celebration or concelebration of the eucharist as a financial necessity or duty. A related factor leading these and other priests to concelebrate or preside daily is the need to reduce Mass obligations incurred by the parish or community, whether or not they need the income from the offerings.

4. **Special occasions.** Many priests, even those who concelebrate infrequently, find it meaningful to concelebrate at special occasions, such as ordinations, celebrations with the bishop, Christmas Midnight Mass, Holy Thursday, Easter Vigil. Many of the faithful experience concelebration, when done properly and with dignity, as lending greater solemnity and importance to a special celebration. It is also seen at times as a way of honoring a person or festivity, such as at first Masses, anniversaries, funerals.

An ontological notion of priesthood, a priestly spirituality stressing the centrality of daily celebration of eucharist, and the Mass-offering system are all factors that strongly motivate priests to preside at or concelebrate the eucharist every day.

Those influenced by all three factors are especially apt to want to preside at or concelebrate every Mass they attend, and they may look on any restrictions on the number of concelebrants as an affront to their dignity. A few even think concelebration is a right to which they are entitled and they highly resent any infringement of this supposed right.

Those who critique or restrict concelebration appear to be in direct conflict with a priestly piety that was predominant in the Latin rite since the Middle Ages until new or recovered theologies of liturgy, ministry and spirituality eroded this consensus in recent decades. A tendency of all social life, including life in the church, is for persons on both sides of any conflict to look to law and legal arguments to support their positions. Canon law cannot be expected to have easy answers to all ecclesial disagreements; this is true of concelebration. However, an awareness of relevant laws from the Code of Canon Law and the Roman Missal can illuminate some of the fundamental issues and this knowledge can become a basis for greater agreement on practice.

At the outset it must be clarified that there is no legal right to concelebrate.[4] In fact, canon 902 states the opposite prerogative, namely, that each priest is free to celebrate individually, provided at least one other member of the faithful is participating (canon 906), although not at the time of a concelebrated Mass in the same church. Thus, no priest can be compelled to concelebrate at any time (apart from his ordination Mass), nor is there any provision in universal law guaranteeing him the right to concelebrate whenever he wishes. On the contrary, the law itself prohibits concelebration whenever "the welfare of the faithful requires or advises otherwise" (canon 902).

The law mandates concelebration in only two cases. According to the General Instruction of the Roman Missal, which is the chief source of universal law on this issue,[5] concelebration is required at the ordination of presbyters and bishops and at the Chrism Mass. This does not mean that all priests present must concelebrate, but that there must be at least some concelebrants in addition to the presiding bishop. The General Instruction further *recommends* several occasions when concelebration would be fitting: (1) the evening Mass of

Holy Thursday; (2) the Mass for councils, meetings of bishops and synods; (3) the Mass for the blessing of an abbot; (4) the conventual Mass that is celebrated in certain religious communities and the principal Mass in churches and oratories; (5) the Mass at any kind of meeting of priests, whether secular or religious. It seems clear from the nature of these occasions that the twin values of the unity of the church and the unity of the presbyterate is the rationale behind the recommendation that Mass be concelebrated.

Although there is no absolute right to concelebrate, is it legally permissible to exclude concelebration apart from ordinations and the Chrism Mass? It seems the answer must be affirmative. GIRM, 155 states that the bishop, in accord with the law, has the right to regulate concelebration in his diocese. In the absence of diocesan guidelines, it falls to the bishop's representatives in the local communities (notably pastors, religious superiors and their collaborators) to regulate con-celebration as they see fit. Nothing in universal law prevents them from deciding that Mass will not be concelebrated or that the number of concelebrants is to be limited. Indeed, canon 902 explicitly supports these decisions insofar as they are motivated by the welfare of the faithful.

Theoretically, a bishop could enact a local law establishing a "right to concelebrate" in the diocese, provided it did not conflict with provisions of universal law and with other rights, such as the legitimate autonomy of religious institutes or the right of a priest to celebrate individually. However, such a diocesan law would be exceedingly impractical because the size of churches and the diversity of liturgical situations and other variables would often make it impossible for all priests to exercise their right without serious aesthetical and logistical problems. The law would also be imprudent and divisive, given the current divergence of viewpoints on the nature of the ministerial priesthood and on other, often emotionally charged issues, such as women's ordination, which can be evoked on the occasion of a concelebrated Mass.

Rather than looking to universal law or new local legislation for the final answer to disagreements on concelebration, it would be better for persons on each side of the issue to try to understand the views and feelings of those on the other side in order to reach general consensus on the frequency and regulation of the practice. Extreme positions on either side may have to be moderated and compromises may have to be made. At times, especially in situations where concelebration may be offensive to or disliked by a significant part of the assembly, both prudence and the welfare of the faithful suggest that arrangements be made for the eucharist to be celebrated by one priest and assisted by one deacon, if available, and by as many laity as are needed for the other liturgical ministries.

Conversely, at special occasions when there is a popular desire for concelebration, such as certain funerals, major feasts and those celebrations mandated or recommended by law for concelebration, those who prepare the liturgy might try to make the most of the symbolic value of concelebration as a sign of the unity of the presbyterate by carefully orchestrating a dignified celebration that maintains liturgical and aesthetical values. In a time of transition in the church from old ideas and practices to new ones, it takes much patience, understanding and charity on the part of everyone to preserve the unity of the church that is meant to be signified and fostered preeminently by the eucharist.

Notes

[1] See, e.g., John F. Baldovin, "Concelebration: A Problem of Symbolic Roles in the Church," *Worship* 59 (1985) 32-47; Robert Taft, "Ex Oriente Lux? Some Reflections on Eucharistic Concelebration," *Worship* 54 (1980) 308-24; R. Kevin Seasoltz, *New Liturgy, New Laws* (Collegeville: Liturgical Press, 1980) 87-90; Aidan Kavanagh, *Elements of Rite: A Handbook of Liturgical Style* (New York: Pueblo, 1982) 13.

[2] *Environment and Art in Catholic Worship,* 12 (Washington DC: USCC, 1978).

[3] GIRM, 170; "Guidelines for the Concelebration of the Eucharist," in *BCL Newsletter* 23 (1987) 37.

[4] See John Huels, "Restrictions on Concelebration," *The Jurist* 47 (1987) 576-78; James Provost, "Some Distinctions on Concelebration," ibid., 579-80.

[5] See nn. 76, 153-208, especially n. 153.

Mass Intentions

At celebrations of the eucharist in parishes and elsewhere, there is a diversity of practices connected with the publicity of intentions for which Mass offerings, formerly called stipends, have been accepted. Sometimes the intention is announced before the Mass begins either by the commentator or the presider. In other places the intention is mentioned during the prayers of the faithful, before or during the eucharistic prayer or at the announcements. The expressions one hears are also various: "This Mass is being offered for Jane Doe," or "especially offered," or "celebrated for." Others include: "The intention of this Mass is . . ." or "The special intention is . . ." In some places the donor of the Mass offering is given a particular role in the liturgy, such as bringing up the bread and wine at the preparation of the gifts. A rather widespread practice is the listing of the Mass intentions in the parish bulletin.

Not all of these practices are conducive to the nature and

ends of the reformed rite of the eucharist and, in fact, can be harmful to them. Which practices are tolerable and which are to be avoided? Before separating the "sheep from the goats," it would be useful to see what implications for pastoral practice can be drawn from the church's new understanding of Mass offerings as reflected in the revised Code of Canon Law.

Mass Offerings in the Revised Code

One of the less-publicized but nevertheless significant developments in the 1983 Code of Canon Law is a revised treatment of Mass offerings. Perhaps the most important change from the old law is that of the title of this institute. No longer are the donations for the application of Mass for a certain intention to be called "stipends" but rather "offerings." The word "stipend" *(stipendium)* in Roman times was used for the wage paid to soldiers. Thomas Aquinas preferred this term for the donation for the celebration of Mass according to a definite intention because it indicated that the donation was compensation for the priest's time and labor rather than the selling of graces. In other words, "stipend" conveys the meaning of payment for services rendered.

The revised code rejects this terminology and instead speaks of an "offering" *(stips)*, a term which better conveys the freewill, gratuitous nature of a gift. Canon 946, which is new to the revised code, states that by giving a Mass offering the faithful "contribute to the good of the church and by their offering take part in the concern of the church for the support of its ministers and works." A Mass offering therefore should be seen as a gift to the church for the support of its ministers or other purposes and not as a contract involving services in return for the payment of money. By accepting a Mass offering the only obligation the priest undertakes is the canonical obligation to celebrate the Mass. When the priest has at least the habitual and implicit intention of offering the Masses at which he presides or concelebrates for the donors' intentions, this obligation is satisfied. No other obligations—such as publicizing the intention—are incurred by accepting the offering.

This and other changes in the revised law's treatment of Mass offerings necessitates a new understanding on the part of the faithful, and especially on the part of priests, about the nature, purpose and quite limited role of Mass offerings and intentions.

Background and Theologies

The practice of accepting a single offering for each Mass in return for the priest's praying for that intention arose in the Middle Ages in response to pastoral need. In this period the faithful were increasingly isolated from the liturgical action and became largely passive spectators of the sacred mysteries being enacted in the sanctuary. The reception of communion was infrequent; the chalice was withheld from the people; clerics or servers took the part of the congregation in responding to the celebrant; even the language of the eucharist was incomprehensible. One of the few ways in which the people could take a more active role was through the Mass stipend system. By making an offering to the priest they were assured that their special intentions would be remembered at the sacrifice.

With the liturgical reforms following Vatican II, however, there is no longer any real need for this kind of participation. The congregation has ample opportunity to participate actively through prayer, song, gesture and acclamation. In particular, the prayers of the faithful at the conclusion of the liturgy of the word accomplish far more effectively the original purpose of the stipend system because these prayers become the joint intentions of the entire worshiping community and not the intention of the priest and donor alone.

This does not mean that Mass offerings no longer have any value or role. If this were true, people would no longer give such offerings, but it is well known that in many countries they remain very popular and there is frequently a surplus of offerings in parishes. The Mass offering system still has a certain appeal on the human level, even though its significance has been greatly diminished by a reformed liturgy and contemporary theology.

Several reasons for this continued appeal of Mass offerings and intentions can be identified: (1) giving a Mass card and making a donation to the church on behalf of a deceased person is a meaningful way for many Catholics to express a message of sympathy to the bereaved; (2) making an offering for a Mass to be applied for a deceased loved one is a way for mourners to feel they are doing something beneficial for the deceased and it provides an opportunity to memorialize the dead publicly; (3) making a donation that is conjoined with the celebration of Mass is a way of concretizing one's prayer to God for a certain intention, much like lighting a votive candle.

These motives are all legitimate. By contrast, the old theological rationale for the Mass stipend system has been severely critiqued by contemporary theologians, such as Karl Rahner, and more recently by liturgists such as M. Francis Mannion and Timothy Fitzgerald.[1] The prevailing theology of Mass stipends in past centuries is attributed in its origins to Duns Scotus (1265?-1308) and other medieval theologians.[2] Scotus postulated a theory of the threefold fruits of the Mass of which one special fruit could be applied by the priest for his intention. The other two fruits, or graces, were for all the faithful and for the priest himself.

Although this theory was widely held in the church for centuries, it is not *de fide*. Indeed, there is no explicit mention of this theology in recent magisterial pronouncements on Mass stipends, namely, in the revised code and in the theological and juridical treatment of Mass stipends in a 1974 apostolic letter of Pope Paul VI.[3] While not rejecting the old theory outright, neither the new code of John Paul II nor the apostolic letter of Paul VI recommended it. On the contrary, these texts indicate that the principal beneficiary of Mass offerings is the church itself, which gains financially, and the secondary beneficiaries are the donors who profit as a result of their spiritual disposition and actual participation in the eucharist and their sharing in the work and ministry of the church.[4]

Neither Paul VI nor the code reinforces the traditional view that there are spiritual benefits or a "special fruit" accruing to the donor's intention as a result of having a Mass applied for it. This is not to suggest that an all-merciful God would not look kindly on the donor's intention, but it does suggest that the contemporary church may be uneasy about guaranteeing special graces from the Mass that the priest can distribute as he will—a guarantee that, in return for the payment of money, is highly suggestive of simony.

A New Praxis

The new understanding of Mass offerings should, on one level, make priests feel less guilty about accepting them and behaving as if they have to provide some kind of special services to earn their wage. A Mass offering can be seen as a donation to the church in memory of some person or intention and nothing more. When a person gives an offering for the celebration of Mass, it can be seen as similar to lighting a votive candle, a way of concretizing one's prayer with an offering to the church or a way of remembering a person by making a donation in that person's name. Provided the Mass obligation is actually satisfied by the priest through the celebration or concelebration of Mass, the priest has no other canonical obligation to fulfill for the donor.

Since Mass offerings and intentions have a very limited part to play in the participative role of the faithful at eucharist, the manner in which these intentions are publicized should not magnify and thereby distort their role to the detriment of the communal nature of the liturgy. Among the practices which have crept into the liturgy, the following especially should be avoided.

1. **Announcing the offering intention before or at some point during the eucharist,** whether this is done with a simple statement of the intention or whether one uses such words as, "This Mass is being offered for . . ." This practice suggests that the principal beneficiary of the eucharistic celebration is the donor's intention. It also creates the impression that the intentions of the worshiping community actually present are somehow less significant than the intention of a donor who may or may not be present.

2. **Isolating the offering intention during the prayers of the faithful.** This is done by praying for the intention and adding the words, "for whom this Mass is offered" or "especially offered." To say that a Mass is offered especially for one intention may be valid

on the human level, as when a particular group gathers in memory of someone and celebrates eucharist. Such memorials meet a human need and are frequently enacted in other contexts, such as a memorial concert. However, to announce routinely that the Mass is offered for one intention, especially that of an anonymous donor who often is not present, is alien to the communitarian nature of the liturgy and again suggests that the intentions of the worshipers actually present are less important.

The liturgy itself indicates that the eucharist is offered for many intentions, not just the intention of the priest. The eucharistic prayers explicitly state that the Mass is offered for the church, the pope, bishops, clergy, faithful, etc. Are these intentions of the whole church any less "special" than the particular intention of the priest?

3. **Naming the offering intention in the eucharistic prayer.** Some priests habitually name the offering intention during the mementos for the living or the dead in the first eucharistic prayer or they use the special mementos for the dead in the second and third prayers. Although this is not illicit, it disproportionately emphasizes the priest's intention. It should be recalled that in the former rite of Mass the canon was prayed quietly and the congregation heard no mention of a name at the memento of the dead. Now that the eucharistic prayers are said aloud in the vernacular, the prayerful participation of the whole worshiping community could be fostered better if the priest, when using the first eucharistic prayer, simply paused briefly and silently mentioned his own intentions. Such a brief pause would in turn encourage the members of the congregation to pray quietly for their own intentions for the living and the deceased. The special mementos of the dead in the second and third eucharistic prayers are best reserved for funeral Masses when the assembly is gathered specifically to pray for one deceased person in particular.

4. **Reserving special roles for the Mass-offering donor,** such as bringing up the gifts in the procession. There is nothing liturgically wrong with such a practice, but it fosters the impression that the Mass-offering donors have special

prerogatives that other worshipers do not enjoy and that the donors have a right to these prerogatives because they paid for them.

Behind all these practices may be lurking the desire to render some service in return for the offering, something beyond the canonical satisfaction of the Mass obligation. Even though in some cases there may be pastoral benefits from these practices, in the end they contribute to a theology of Mass offerings that is ill-suited to the reformed liturgy. Moreover, such practices suggest that people who give a Mass offering are entitled to special goods or services in exchange for their payment. It is hard to defend against the charge that the Mass offering system is inherently simoniacal when special consideration in the liturgy can be bought for five dollars or whatever the established offering may be.

Pastoral Recommendations

Some have suggested that the best way to eradicate the bad theology and simoniacal associations connected with Mass offerings and intentions is to abolish the system altogether,[5] but this is not likely to happen soon. In lieu of this solution the practices mentioned above should be halted because they foster misconceptions and are ill-suited to the reformed liturgy.

Certain practices may be maintained without detriment to the liturgy or to the new understanding of the proper role of Mass offerings and intentions.

1. **Publishing the offering intentions in the parish bulletin.** This practice encourages the entire community to pray for an intention without giving it a disproportionate role in the liturgical action itself.

2. **Praying for the offering intention along with other intentions of the same category in the prayers of the faithful.** For example, if the intention is for a deceased person, this person could be mentioned along with other deceased persons being prayed for at that moment. However, one should not add "for whom this Mass is offered," since it reflects an outdated theology and fosters the impression that it is the only significant intention of the Mass.

The performance of either or both of these practices is more than what is required. Canon law specifies only that the Mass obligation be satisfied, but it does not require any publicity of this fact other than accurate bookkeeping. When the offering intention is treated at liturgy in its properly diminutive role, the liturgy will communicate more effectively the contemporary understanding of the Mass offering as a gift to the church and not as the payment for special favors or graces.

Notes

[1]Rahner, "Multiplication of Masses," *Orate Fratres* 24 (1950) 553-62; Rahner and Angelus Häussling, *The Celebration of the Eucharist* (New York: Herder and Herder, 1968) 114-25; Mannion, "Stipends and Eucharistic Praxis," in *Living Bread, Saving Cup,* ed. R. Kevin Seasoltz (Collegeville: Liturgical Press, 1987) 324-46; Fitzgerald, "The Story of the Stipend," Part I: *Liturgy 80* 16 (October 1985) 2-5; Part II: ibid. (November/December 1985) 7-9; Part III: *Liturgy 80* 17 (January 1986) 2-4.

[2]See Gilbert Ostdiek, "The Threefold Fruits of the Mass: Notes and Reflections on Scotus' Quodlibetal Questions, q. 20," in *Essays Honoring Allan B. Wolter,* ed. William A. Frank and Girard J. Etzkorn (St. Bonaventure, NY: Franciscan Institute Publications, 1985) 201-19; and Edward Kilmartin, "The One Fruit or the Many Fruits of the Mass," *Proceedings of the Catholic Theological Society of America* 21 (1966) 37-68.

[3]Apostolic letter *motu proprio, Firma in traditione,* June 13, 1974, AAS 66 (1974) 308-11; DOL, 2234.

[4]For an explanation of this conclusion, see John Huels, "Stipends in the New Code of Canon Law," in *Living Bread, Saving Cup,* loc. cit., 347-56; also found in idem, *One Table, Many Laws: Essays on Catholic Eucharistic Practice* (Collegeville: Liturgical Press, 1986) chapter 7.

[5]For references to those who express this viewpoint, see Fitzgerald, loc. cit., Part III, 3-4, especially note 53.

Reducing the Number of Masses

                In recent years there has been an effort on the part of officials in some dioceses to try to reduce the number of Sunday Masses in parishes. In the archdiocese of Chicago, for example, Cardinal Joseph Bernardin noted "the unnecessarily large numbers of Sunday Masses celebrated in some parishes and how this adversely affects the quality of liturgy."[1] The archdiocese has issued guidelines that include a directive to eliminate or combine with other Masses those Sunday Masses at which the attendance is consistently less than 50 percent of the capacity.[2] Exceptions are permitted for multilingual and multicultural parishes and those buildings too large for the small number of active parishioners. In the latter case, the guidelines call for a reexamination of the worship space.

The principal reason behind such diocesan policies is to promote better liturgical celebrations. Several specific factors related to the promotion of good liturgy are mentioned in one way or another in policy statements on this issue:

Participation in song, responses and common prayer is better in a full or nearly full church than in one where individuals are isolated and scattered; priests are more likely to approach the Sunday eucharist with greater prayerfulness and enthusiasm when their presidency is not required at too many Masses on a weekend; the reduction in the number of unnecessary Masses allows a better utilization of lay ministers and other resources.

In this essay we shall see that diocesan efforts to reduce the number of Masses in order to enhance the quality of Sunday liturgy are supported by the Apostolic See, both in canon law and in sections of other liturgical documents. Besides the Code of Canon Law, we shall also consider chiefly the 1967 instruction of the Congregation of Rites on the worship of the eucharist, *Eucharisticum mysterium,*[3] and the 1969 instruction of the Congregation for Divine Worship on Masses with special groups, *Actio pastoralis.*[4] The discussion will develop four noteworthy points made in *Eucharisticum mysterium,* 25-27:

1. The sense of ecclesial community should be carefully developed by the experience of Sunday Mass. The locus of Sunday worship should be the cathedral and the parish churches.

2. Small religious communities should attend the local parish on Sunday. Masses for other small groups also should be held on weekdays so that the unity of the parish community may be manifest in the Sunday and holy day eucharist.

3. It is highly desirable to promote the active participation of all the people in the Sunday celebration. This is expressed above all in singing. As far as is possible, the sung form of celebration is preferred.

4. The number of Masses is not to be so multiplied as to harm pastoral effectiveness so that churches are underutilized or priests are overworked.

The Experience of Sunday

The celebration of the paschal mysteries on Sunday, the Lord's Day, is, according to Vatican II, "a tradition handed down from the apostles which has its origin from the very day of Christ's resurrection."[5] The primacy and centrality of Sunday among the days and feasts of the year is a basic emphasis of the contemporary liturgical reform. Sunday is the "primordial holy day"[6] when the entire church gathers to celebrate its faith in Christ. The Sunday eucharist is the principal celebration of the gathered church; it both signifies the unity of believers and also fosters that unity.

If this unity is to be signified and fostered effectively, the Sunday eucharistic liturgy should truly be a celebration of the whole community. This cannot be realized when the parish community is scattered about in an underused church at too many needless Masses.

A related issue, one also addressed in diocesan policies on the number of Sunday Masses, is that of the Saturday evening, "anticipated" Mass of Sunday. Some dioceses have adopted a policy forbidding more than one anticipated Mass in any parish. Saturday evening Masses were originally intended principally for people who were unable to participate on Sundays due to work, travel, etc. Pastors were supposed to "take steps to prevent in any way the lessening of the sense of what Sunday is" (EM, 28). However, many attend the vigil Mass simply as a way of fulfilling their obligation early. Consequently, the special, sacred character of Sunday is frequently lost and the Lord's Day becomes a day not only free from work, but also free from worship.

Small Group Masses

Special Masses should not be celebrated for small groups on Sundays. This is specifically prohibited in *Actio pastoralis,* except in particular cases, "lest the parish liturgical assembly be deprived of that ministry of priests and participation of the people which would benefit the life and unity of the community" (AP, 10, a). If special groups cannot gather for Mass on a weekday, they should be incorporated in a regularly scheduled Sunday liturgy (EM, 27). Thus, it might be feasible occasionally to celebrate baptisms, weddings, anniversaries, gatherings of members of an organization, etc., at the Sunday eucharist.

Masses for special groups, such as parish organizations, families or school children, can pose a problem on weekdays as well, because parish priests frequently must preside at more than one Mass on a weekday due to funerals, weddings and other events. As will be seen, canon law prohibits priests from celebrating more than one or two Masses on weekdays that are not holy days, including Saturdays.

Even when it is possible to celebrate Mass on a weekday for a special group, *Actio pastoralis* says that it is necessary to ensure that "no Mass is to be regarded as a celebration belonging exclusively to a particular group, but as the celebration of the church" (AP, 5, b). Moreover, in his homily at a special group Mass the priest is always supposed "to explain the relationships existing between the assembly presently gathered and the local and universal church" (AP, 6, g). This is in keeping with the fundamental principle enunciated at Vatican II that the liturgy is not a private function but a celebration of the whole church (SC, 26).

Often groups request a eucharistic celebration simply because they are most familiar with it. However, the Apostolic See has stated that the eucharist may not always be advantageous or advisable in small group settings and other forms of worship would be more fitting (AP, 1). With the decline of popular devotions following Vatican II, many Catholics scarcely know of any kind of communal prayer other than eucharist. They need to be taught and encouraged to experience other forms of prayer and liturgy, especially the liturgy of the hours and services of the word. These services can be conducted by deacons and lay leaders as well as priests; they provide an experience of communal prayer that is often what the special groups are primarily seeking; they also help to maintain the eucharist as a celebration of parish unity which is open to all and not just to the members of some family, group or organization.

Many parishes prohibit all special eucharistic liturgies for small groups on Sundays. No exceptions are allowed, even for marriages, anniversaries or parish organizations. This is a good policy, both theologically and practically. Theologically, it helps to maintain the centrality of the Sunday eucharist which signifies and fosters the unity of the parish community.

Practically, it helps to minimize the number of Sunday Masses at which priests must preside, so that they are able to preside more effectively when they must.

It is gratifying to see how many religious communities, even clerical communities, have responded well to the call of *Eucharisticum mysterium* to celebrate the paschal mysteries on Sunday together with their fellow Christians in the local parish. Religious serve in and belong to the local church, so it is desirable that they share their presence and talents with their brothers and sisters in the parish church or diocesan cathedral on the Lord's day rather than observe it separately in their own houses. Unless a religious house has a large number of members, especially many who are infirm and unable to be taken to the local parish, it would be in keeping with the mind of the church not to have eucharist there on Sundays.

Active Participation

Another fundamental principle of the liturgical reform is the "full, conscious and active participation" of all the people.[7] When too few people attend a Sunday eucharist, their participation suffers. Thus, the Cardinal Secretary of State Giovanni Villot, speaking on behalf of Pope Paul VI in 1977, urged "a reduction, if necessary, of the number of Masses in order that, avoiding division and dispersion, the formation of well-attended assemblies may be encouraged, whose members are familiar with one another."[8]

Church documents stress the importance of music and singing in bringing about the full and active participation of all. In addition to *Eucharisticum mysterium,* cited above, other noteworthy documents treating liturgical music include the Constitution on the Liturgy of Vatican II, especially nn. 112-121; the 1967 instruction of the Congregation of Rites, *Musicam sacram,* on music in the liturgy;[9] and the 1972 statement of the Bishops' Committee on the Liturgy, Music in Catholic Worship, together with its 1982 supplement, Liturgical Music Today.[10]

Since the role of music and singing is a principal expression of the full and active participation in the liturgy of all the faithful, it is not surprising that the church desires fewer Masses on Sundays when they are not needed. The quality of the participation, especially singing, is nearly always better in a full church than amid a congregation dispersed about a spacious nave.

With fewer Sunday Masses, the quality of participation should improve because it becomes possible to make better use of resources; planning and preparation are also facilitated. Many parishes lack enough volunteers to have choir or cantors at every Mass. Some pastors claim that they cannot get enough eucharistic ministers to offer the cup at every Mass. Some parishes lack enough lectors who read well, and/or enough ushers, altar servers and other ministers. With fewer Masses and more people present at them, it is easier to ensure that at every Sunday Mass there will be good music and strong participation, communion under both kinds, and enough well-prepared ministers for all the liturgical roles and functions.

Effect on Priests

Eucharisticum mysterium mentions the negative effect on priests of presiding at multiple Masses on the same day. Many priests find that it is difficult to remain fresh and enthusiastic after two Masses. When the president of the assembly lacks energy, when he is tired or bored, when he really would prefer not to be at one more eucharist that weekend, it is not unusual for the people in the congregation to sense this. As a result, they do not feel invited or encouraged to give their own full and active participation.

The church's discipline has traditionally forbidden the priest from celebrating more than one Mass a day. The present law, in canon 905, continues this tradition. The canon begins by stating that "it is not licit for a priest to celebrate the eucharist more than once a day except for certain instances [such as Christmas] when the law permits such celebration or concelebration more than once." After establishing this rule, the second paragraph states an exception: "If priests are lacking, the local Ordinary may permit priests, for a just cause, to celebrate twice a day and even, if pastoral need requires it, three times on Sundays and holy days of obligation."

The permission to binate can be granted only when priests are lacking and for a just cause. The permission to trinate further requires pastoral necessity. These conditions indicate that there must be some good reason of a pastoral nature for binating and a real necessity for trinating. The mere convenience of the people is not a necessity. Ordinarily such necessity would be demonstrated only when there are too many people who wish to attend Mass and not enough priests and space in the church to accommodate them. When churches are significantly underutilized and can hold considerably more people on Sundays, clearly the proper response to the law is to reduce the number of Masses rather than to use the local Ordinary's permission to binate or trinate without adequate reason.

Overcoming Resistance to Change

The attempt to reduce the number of Sunday Masses frequently meets with resistance on the part of some pastors who prefer to retain schedules developed in the past when Mass attendance was higher. The reasons for maintaining a needlessly large number of Masses are various, but they generally have little to do with the quality of the liturgical celebration.

The most common reasons expressed are the fear of displeasing the people who will think the priests are lazy and not giving them service, and the fear that people will go elsewhere and the collection will decline. One pastor confided that he will not reduce his Mass schedule because he is afraid the bishop will take away one of his assistant priests. Underlying these fears is often the notion of Sunday Mass as primarily an obligation rather than a festive celebration of God's people gathered in praise and thanksgiving in memory of the paschal mysteries. If Sunday eucharist is perceived by a pastor chiefly as an obligation rather than a celebration, he might provide more Masses than are needed because he believes he is offering a true service to his parishioners by making the fulfillment of their obligation as convenient as possible.

Experience has shown that the objects of these fears rarely materialize when the Mass schedule is altered. Surely, some parishioners may initially be disturbed by a change in schedule, but they quickly get used to attending Mass at a new time. Human beings, even those of a conservative nature, are quite adaptable and can readily make adjustments in their life when necessary. Many people even enjoy having their weekly routines altered from time to time. Moreover, most parishioners have a sense of loyalty to their parish and will not fail to support and attend it merely because the Mass schedule has been changed.

The fear that the people will think the priests are not giving them good service is ironic indeed. On the contrary, the purpose of reducing the number of unnecessary Masses is precisely to improve the quality of the liturgy. This is in the real interest of the people. It is not a true service to the people to offer sparsely attended Masses for their mere convenience, as if the church were like a discount store or fast-food chain with a competitive product to sell to volatile consumers.

It seems that the principal reason why people attend Mass at a parish other than their own is because the liturgy, preaching and experience of community are better there than at their own parish, not because the time for Mass is more convenient. An exception is the late Sunday afternoon or evening Mass, offered by relatively few parishes, which attracts people from different areas primarily because of the unique time it is offered. However, it is a common observation that these late Sunday Masses generally have the worst participation. This is not surprising. People coming together from various parishes merely to fulfill their Sunday obligation have little sense of community or belonging and rarely feel comfortable as active participants in the singing and communal prayer.

While the pastor may be convinced of the desirability of reducing the number of Masses, he may encounter resistance on the part of parish council or parishioners at large. To overcome any potential resistance, it is desirable, before any change is made, to educate the parish about the values at stake, particularly the liturgical values. The archdiocese of Chicago has provided bulletin inserts for this purpose, and this kind of approach can be augmented by special meetings and explanations from the pulpit. Some pastors have reported success in introducing a schedule change when they have preceded it by a general survey of the parishioners to determine what times for Masses in a new schedule they would prefer. This makes the people a part of the decision; they are then much less likely to blame the pastor, staff or parish council if they do not like the new schedule.

The excessive number of Sunday Masses might seem a trifling problem among the many pressing demands that pastors must face every day. But it is not. The Sunday eucharist is the center, the spiritual heart of the parish; in the words of Vatican II, it is "the font and apex of the whole Christian life."[11] Since the eucharist is basic to the identity of the church itself, any effort to increase the quality of the people's participation at eucharist must rank among the most important tasks of the pastoral ministry.

Notes

[1]*Our Communion, Our Peace, Our Promise: Pastoral Letter on the Liturgy* (Chicago: Liturgy Training Publications, 1984) 21.

[2]Sunday Mass Guidelines, Archdiocese of Chicago, 1985.

[3]May 25, 1967, AAS 59 (1969) 539-73; DOL, 1230.

[4]May 15, 1969, AAS 61 (1969) 806-11; DOL, 2120.

[5]SC, 106.

[6]SC, 106; EM, 25; CIC, canon 1246.

[7]See, e.g., SC, 14, 19, 21, 30, 41, 48 and 50.

[8]Address to the Italian National Liturgical Week, *Notitiae* 13 (1977) 470-71; *BCL Newsletter* 13 (December 1977) 1.

[9]March 5, 1967, AAS 60 (1967) 300-20; DOL, 4122.

[10]Both are published by the USCC, Washington DC.

[11]Dogmatic Constitution on the Church, *Lumen gentium,* 11, November 21, 1964, AAS 57 (1965) 5-67.

First Confession

Among the most disputed pastoral and canonical questions in the decades following Vatican II is whether the first confession of young children can be celebrated after their first communion. In the early 1960s, some parishes began to postpone first confession until a year or two after first communion. By the early 1970s, more than half the parishes in the United States had adopted this practice.[1] Since there was no church law at the time prescribing first confession before first communion, pastors were at liberty to accept the arguments of psychologists, religious educators, theologians and others that children were more likely to benefit from individual confession, and also less likely to be disturbed by it, at a somewhat later age than seven, which is the standard age for reception of first communion in the Latin church.

However, with the appearance of the revised Code of Canon Law in 1983, new questions were raised about the legality of this practice due to a phrase, given here in italics, that was inserted in canon 914, which treats preparation for first communion. Canon 914 states:

> It is the responsibility, in the first place, of parents and those who take the place of parents as well as of the pastor to see that children who have reached the use of reason are correctly prepared and are nourished by the divine food as early as possible, *preceded by sacramental confession;* it is also for the pastor to be vigilant lest any children come to the Holy Banquet who have not reached the use of reason or whom he judges are not sufficiently disposed.

Before considering the meaning of this phrase, it will be useful to set the context by presenting some of the chief reasons in favor of and against celebrating first penance after first communion.

Reasons for Penance after Communion

The reasons in favor of the first penance of young children after first communion have come from various viewpoints, including theological, historical, psychological and catechetical. Theologians point out that the original, normative sequence for reception of the sacraments, as witnessed in the Rite of Christian Initiation of Adults, is baptism first, confirmation second, eucharist third, and then other sacraments when needed or desired. Indeed, for the first 12 centuries infants received first communion at their baptism in the Latin church, a practice still found in Eastern churches.

Moral theologians and others, reflecting on the findings of developmental psychology, have concluded that children are incapable of the necessary discretion and maturity to commit mortal sin, and the Council of Trent only required that *mortal* sins be confessed individually and integrally.[2] The church recognizes other ways of obtaining pardon for venial sin besides sacramental absolution, including worthy participation in the eucharist itself. Although children are capable of committing venial sin, various authorities on child development assert that the normal child is not mature enough to appreciate the genuine nature of sin and the meaning of forgiveness and reconciliation in the church until about the age of nine or ten. Further, they claim that it is only by about the fourth grade that children usually have developed a consciousness of belonging to and depending on a social group, and this consciousness is necessary for appreciating the social aspect of sin and reconciliation.[3]

There are also pedagogical reasons for returning to the more-ancient practice of initiation into the eucharist before first penance. Many religious educators maintain that when first penance occurs a year or two after first communion, teachers are better able to provide adequate catechesis in preparation for each sacrament. They also observe that children at a somewhat older age than seven have less fear of individual confession and are able to approach the sacrament with greater understanding and freedom and a more mature faith. Consequently, the required proper disposition for the sacrament can better be assured. This factor is all the more significant with the new Rite of Penance published in 1974. This requires a more intense degree of personal involvement by the penitents in the celebration of individual reconciliation than was demanded by the previous rite.

Reasons for Penance First

Several reasons for continuing the pre-Vatican II practice of delaying first communion until after first penance have been given by certain authorities of the Roman curia. The principal reason appears to be the protection of the right of children to receive the sacrament of penance. This insistence on the right to the sacrament apparently resulted from complaints received by the Holy See from parents and others who said that in some parishes children were refused absolution by priests or were impeded from receiving the sacrament by teachers of religion.[4] If children who have the use of reason are refused the sacrament of penance, they are denied a right to which they are entitled by law.

Another reason for first penance before first communion is pedagogical. In a December 20, 1986, letter, Cardinal Augustine Mayer, the prefect of the Congregation for the Sacraments, described the "formative and pastoral aim" of canon 914, "that is, to educate [children] from a tender age to the true Christian spirit of penance and conversion, to growth in self-knowledge and self-control, to the just sense of sin, even of venial sin, to the necessity of asking for pardon of God and above all to a loving and confident abandonment to the mercy of the Lord."[5]

Another reason the Holy See has given for penance before first communion has to do with the efficaciousness of sacramental penance which, even in the case of venial sins, "gives an increase of grace and of charity, increases the child's good dispositions for receiving the eucharist, and also helps to perfect the Christian life."[6] One might look to M. Francis Mannion's distinction between "penance" and "reconciliation" as support for this view. According to Mannion, penance consists of all the acts of Christians in their ongoing process of conversion and moral transformation; reconcilation is the overcoming of a radical break with God and the church brought about by serious sin.[7] While little children do not need the sacrament of penance for "reconciliation" for serious sin, they could benefit from it as a form of penitential act.

A final reason given by the Holy See for celebrating first penance before first communion concerns the "need for safeguarding and protecting worthy participation in the eucharist."[8] This view holds that, without prior sacramental confession, the pastor is not able to judge whether a child has the proper disposition to receive holy communion.

Interpretation of Canon 914

Having briefly looked at some reasons given in favor of and against having first communion of young children before their first confession, we must now address the question of the legality of the practice. One way of looking at the issue is to ask whether first communion can be denied to any child who does not wish to approach the sacrament of penance.

The law itself indicates a negative answer to this question. Canon 913 is relevant on this point. It treats the minimal requirements for the administration of the eucharist to children and it makes no mention of penance. In order to make first communion, children ordinarily must "have sufficient knowledge and careful preparation so as to understand the mystery of Christ according to their capacity" and they must be able to "receive the body of Christ with faith and devotion." In danger of death, however, they only need to be "able to distinguish the body of Christ from ordinary food and to receive communion reverently." The canon does not say they must have the ability to make an individual, integral confession.

What, then, is the correct interpretation of the phrase "preceded by sacramental confession" in canon 914? According to a standard principle of canonical interpretation, the meaning of a law must be considered in its text and context (canon 17). If one looks carefully at the text and context of canon 914, one observes that its requirements are not directed to children, as they are in the preceding canon. Instead, the obligations and requirements of canon 914 are imposed on parents and the pastor. It is primarily the responsibility of parents, and secondarily that of the pastor, to see that children are properly prepared for first communion—which includes preparation for first penance. It does not seem that the children themselves are explicitly the subject of an obligation to confess before making first communion.

If this interpretation is correct, then children are bound by the same law as are Catholics who are older. This is the law of canon 916, which states that only serious sins must be confessed before the reception of holy communion (unless there is a grave reason and no opportunity of confessing, in which case the person should make an act of perfect contrition, including the intention of confessing as soon as possible). Thus, children who have reached the age of discretion and *who are aware of serious sin* are obliged ordinarily to confess before receiving communion. The confession of venial sins is a recommendation of the law, not a requirement, and this recommendation is not mentioned in connection with reception of first communion (canon 988, §2). Nor should anyone, including children, be coerced against their will to receive the sacrament as this may well affect the necessary freedom and proper disposition required in the recipient.[9]

Seen in its proper context, including the documentation from the Roman curia discussed above, the new phrase inserted in canon 914 evidently is an obligation on parents and pastors to see that children are prepared for the sacrament of penance before first communion so that the children realistically may exercise their right to the sacrament. If there is no preparation, children are effectively denied the right to the sacrament. However, should a child not wish to receive the sacrament of penance, especially when the parents also believe the child is not ready for it, a pastor would not be justified on this basis alone for assuming that a child is not ready for first communion.

Canon law lists among its fundamental rights the right to receive the sacraments (canon 213). Moreover, ministers may not deny the sacraments to those who ask for them at appropriate times, are properly disposed and are not prohibited by law from receiving them (canon 843, §1). Having the proper disposition is thus a requirement for the reception of all sacraments, not just for first communion. In the case of certain other sacraments, such as adult initiation, marriage and holy orders, it is easier for the minister to determine readiness and disposition because the minister or other responsible authority generally interacts with the candidates or recipients on an individual basis and gets to know them to some extent during the course of the preparation for and celebration of the sacrament.

On the other hand, ministers of communion are rarely able to judge the disposition of all those who approach the Lord's table. What priest, deacon or lay minister is able to discern the inner worthiness of all communicants? For the most part, the minister can only presume that the person requesting the eucharist is in good conscience. Only when there are serious reasons for doubting the communicant's worthiness would it be appropriate to deny holy communion, such as when a person has been publicly excommunicated or interdicted (canon 915).

The same caution about denial of the sacrament must be exercised in the case of a doubt about the disposition of first communicants. The mere fact that a young child does not make a prior sacramental confession is not a sufficient reason for suspecting that that child is in a state of mortal sin or lacks sufficient knowledge and preparation for first communion *according to the child's capacity*—which is what canon 913 requires.

It can safely be asserted that a child cannot be denied the right to receive first communion solely because he or she does not wish to approach the sacrament of penance. The requirement of penance before first communion is not absolute; it can admit of exceptions. Nevertheless, as many exceptions as there might be in practice, it would not be licit to establish a general policy permitting penance after first communion that would effectively deny or restrict the access of children to sacramental penance. Parents and pastors are canonically obliged to see that some catechesis on penance is given to children before they make their first communion. However, the actual choice of going to the sacrament must always be primarily that of the individual child while respecting the views of the parents who, "because they have given life to their children . . . have a most serious obligation and enjoy the right to educate them" (canon 226, §2).[10]

A final question merits brief comment: How much preparation for first penance must the parents and pastor (or, in their place, the parish school of religion) provide before first communion? Canon law does not answer this. Clearly, there must be some preparation so that children who wish to confess are able to do so properly and to understand what they are doing according to their capacity. On the other hand, the total catechesis on penance offered by the parish religious education program does not have to be given prior to first communion.

It would be good to recall that, in the early centuries after Christ, catechumens were first sacramentally initiated into the church, and the mystagogy, or instruction on the sacraments, came only after they experienced them. Just as the mystery of the eucharist is continually unfolded through Christian life, liturgy and formation in successive years after first communion, so also one's understanding of the mystery of reconciliation with God and the church is a process that can continually be deepened by further catechesis and liturgical celebrations throughout one's lifetime.[11]

Notes

[1]Thomas F. Sullivan, "The Directory and First Confession," *The Living Light* 16 (1979) 199-200.

[2]Trent, session XIII, *De euch.,* cap. 7, canon 11, DS 1646-47, 1661.

[3]Thomas F. Sullivan, "What Age for First Confession?" *America* 129 (1973) 112; Ladislas Orsy, "The Sins of Those Little Ones," *America* 129 (1973) 438-41.

[4]Congregation for the Sacraments and Divine Worship and Congregation for the Clergy, letter to the conferences of bishops, April 30, 1976. This and other documentation from the Holy See on the issue of first penance is available in *Liturgy Documentary Series 7: Penance and Reconciliation in the Church* (Washington, DC: USCC, 1986) 41-57; DOL, 379-82, 985-91.

[5]Congregation for the Sacraments, letter to Archbishop John May, president of the NCCB, private, prot. n. 1400/86.

[6]Congregation for the Clergy, *General Catechetical Directory,* April 11, 1971, AAS 64 (1972) 97-176, Addendum, n. 5; DOL, 1120.

[7]Mannion, "Penance and Reconciliation: A Systemic Analysis," *Worship* 60 (1986) 109.

[8]Congregation for the Sacraments and Divine Worship and Congregation for the Clergy, letter to the conferences of bishops, *In quibusdam Ecclesiae partibus,* March 31, 1977; DOL, 3149.

[9]See Ellen O'Hara, "Penance and Canon Law," in *Reconciliation: The Continuing Agenda*, ed. Robert J. Kennedy (Collegeville: Liturgical Press, 1987) 245.

[10]For a thorough study of the canonical issues surrounding first penance, see James H. Provost, "The Reception of First Penance," *The Jurist* 47 (1987) 294-340.

[11]See Linda Gaupin, " 'Let Those Who Have Faith Not Be Hasty': Penance and Children," in *Reconciliation: The Continuing Agenda,* especially 231-35.

General
Absolution

Of all the liturgical rites of the Latin church whose revision was mandated by the Second Vatican Council, the rites of penance have likely been the most difficult to implement fully. They remain to varying degrees a source of confusion to clergy and laity alike. Such confusion seems especially to surround the third rite of sacramental penance, the Rite for Reconciliation of Several Penitents with General Confession and Absolution, more frequently called simply "general absolution." On this issue, Pope John Paul II in his Apostolic Exhortation on Reconciliation and Penance said that church law "must be accepted and applied in such a way as to avoid any sort of arbitrary interpretation."[1]

The church's law on general absolution is readily accessible in the Code of Canon Law and the Rite of Penance of the Roman Ritual, but it is not easily understood without some knowledge of canonical principles of interpretation. Law must always be interpreted in some fashion before it can be observed. The problem of "arbitrary interpretation," to use the words of the pope, more easily arises when the law is rather complicated and technical as it is in the case of general absolution.

This essay proposes to interpret the universal law on general absolution from the perspective of a canonist and to give some pastoral indications of how the law can best be observed. The intent is to explain the meaning of the law and exemplify it in order to reveal what opportunities there may be for the use of general absolution and what situations would, conversely, be excluded.

The principal source of confusion with the third rite of penance has to do with the situations in which it is lawful to use general confession and absolution. Some bishops and episcopal conferences maintain that there are never any occasions in their territory when all the conditions of the law can be met, and therefore they urge that general absolution not be used.[2] It is difficult to conceive of an interpretation more arbitrary than this!

It should be obvious from the start that general absolution, introduced in the Roman Ritual by Pope Paul VI, as he asserted, "with our special approval and by our mandate,"[3] is an authentic form of sacramental penance intended to be used as the law permits for the good of the faithful. Indeed, in some places situations of necessity are so frequent that general absolution, although considered an extraordinary means of reconciliation, actually is the rule rather than the exception due to a dearth of confessors and a multitude of penitents.

Conditions for General Absolution

Canon law permits general absolution without previous individual confession in two cases. The first is when danger of death is imminent and there is not enough time for the available priests to hear the confessions of individual penitents (canon 961, §1, 1°). The danger of death should be real, though it need not be certain that the persons are in fact going to die imminently. Soldiers going to battle, for example, are considered to be in danger of death even though many or most may not actually die.

The second case for general absolution is that of serious necessity, namely, "when in light of the number of penitents a supply of confessors is not readily available rightly to hear the confessions of individuals within a suitable time so that the penitents are forced to be deprived of sacramental grace or holy communion for a long time through no fault of their own; it is not considered a sufficient necessity if confessors cannot be readily available only because of the great number of penitents as can occur on the occasion of some great feast or pilgrimage" (canon 961, §1, 2°).

Before examining the key phrases of this law, it will be helpful to explain the distinction between strict and broad interpretation of canon law. Laws that establish a penalty, that restrict rights or that contain an exception to law must be strictly interpreted (canon 10); other laws may be interpreted broadly. In light of clarifications from the Holy See,[4] the discipline on general absolution is properly viewed as exceptional law and thus subject to strict interpretation. Individual confession and absolution of serious sin is the norm; general confession and absolution of serious sin is the exception. Thus, the law on general absolution, at least for those in serious sin, is subject to strict interpretation. This means that all the conditions of the law must be met before general absolution can be celebrated.

On the other hand, a strict interpretation should not be "restrictive." Strict interpretation is literal; it stays within the meaning of the words of the law as they are understood in the canonical tradition. A restrictive interpretation is too strict; it imposes burdens not demanded by the law. A restrictive interpretation of a law would be improper and would amount to the kind of arbitrary interpretation that, the pope said, should be avoided. Moreover, when the meaning of a word or phrase is doubtful or has several interpretations, that interpretation should be preferred which favors the right of the faithful to receive the sacrament.

Key Phrases

Not readily available. This is the first phrase of the law that calls for some interpretative comment. One of the conditions for the use of general absolution is that a supply of confessors is not readily available. This means that they are not there presently, that they cannot be summoned without delay or inconvenience. It does not refer to the total number of confessors in the area or the diocese, but rather to the number of confessors actually present at the time that the sacrament of penance is being celebrated.

Rightly to hear the confessions of individuals. The emphasis should be on "rightly"—*rite* in the Latin—which not only means correctly or properly but also, more literally, means "according to religious ceremonies," "with due religious observances." In other words, when the Rite of Reconciliation of Individual Penitents (Rite 1) or the Rite of Reconciliation of Several Penitents with Individual Confession and Absolution (Rite 2) cannot be fittingly celebrated due to the number of penitents and the shortage of confessors, general absolution may be used when the other conditions of the law are met.

It is not licit outside the danger of death to truncate Rite 1 or 2 by omitting something from the celebration of penance that is not optional in order to save time.[5] One could hardly assert that the mind of the legislator is that confessors should act contrary to ecclesiastical law merely to avoid using Rite 3.

Within a suitable time. This refers to the time necessary to celebrate Rite 1 or 2 with individual confession and absolution. If it cannot be done rightly *(rite),* with all the meanings that implies, within a suitable time, the law permits general absolution when the other conditions are met. The meaning of a "suitable time" can only be understood by the confessor according to local circumstances. What is a suitable time for people in this particular parish or locale? How long can a minister reasonably expect the faithful to wait for the sacrament? If, for example, parishioners assemble for a communal celebration of the sacrament of penance with individual confession and absolution (Rite 2) in a parish where this ordinarily takes about one hour, to keep the people waiting much beyond that time might not be suitable for the people in that place.

Deprived of sacramental grace or holy communion. Absolution of sins is not always necessary before receiving communion, even for those in serious sin, because when there is no opportunity of confessing serious sins individually one can make an act of perfect contrition with the intention of confessing as soon as possible (canon 916). However, absolution is necessary for the grace of the sacrament of penance, and this is what "sacramental grace" refers to in this context. If it is impossible rightly to celebrate Rite 1 or Rite 2 due to the large number of penitents and the lack of sufficient confessors, the penitents would clearly be deprived of the grace of the sacrament.

Even if penitents are not in serious sin, it would not be good pastoral practice for a minister to deprive those who seek sacramental penance from receiving the grace of the sacrament. In fact, it would seem to be unlawful. Canon 213 states a fundamental right of the faithful to receive the sacraments; canon 843, §1 says that ordained ministers cannot refuse the sacraments to those who are properly disposed, who are not prohibited by law from receiving them and who ask for them at appropriate times—and what is a more appropriate time to ask for the sacrament than at a scheduled celebration of the sacrament of penance?

For a long time. The penitents are forced to be deprived of sacramental grace or holy communion for "a long time." The Latin word is *diu,* and the law gives no indication of how long a time this might be. In 1988 the conference of bishops of the United States passed a resolution defining *diu* as "a month."[6] The policy of the Canadian conference of bishops, on the other hand, does not attempt to define *diu* but leaves it to local pastoral judgment according to the circumstances.

Indeed, there is no objective standard for what constitutes a long time for anyone to remain in a state of sin and be deprived of the grace of reconciliation. The canonical tradition has interpreted *diu* relatively; some canonists assert that in a particular case *diu* might be for as short a time as one day.[7] For some persons, to go for even one day without absolution of a serious sin would be a painful burden.

Also regarding the "long time" to be deprived of holy communion, it is not possible, without arbitrariness, to establish an absolute standard that applies to all persons and situations. As seen above, absolution from grave sin is not always necessary before receiving holy communion. Someone in serious sin may receive holy communion without prior confession and absolution by making an act of perfect contrition in accord with canon 916. However, the law specifies that this option be chosen only for a "grave reason." General absolution, on the other hand, can be given in order to permit such persons to receive communion even when they do not have a grave reason for going to communion (other than that they would be deprived of the sacrament for a long time). Moreover, the solution of canon 916 is less satisfactory than general absolution, not only because the grace of the sacrament of penance is lacking, but also because such an act of perfect contrition remains a private act of an individual sinner as opposed to the explicitly ecclesial action of Rite 3.[8]

It would be preferable for local churches to leave it to the confessor to determine what constitutes "a long time" for the penitents according to their needs and the circumstances in the situation at hand. A restrictive, overly scrupulous interpretation of *diu* could easily have the effect of unjustly denying the faithful their right to the sacrament of penance.

No matter how *diu* is understood, the burden falls on pastoral ministers, especially pastors of parishes, to decide whether to use general absolution in a given case. Pastors are canonically obliged "to see to it that the Christian faithful are nourished through a devout celebration of the sacraments and especially that they frequently approach the sacrament of the most holy eucharist and the sacrament of penance" (canon 528, §2). The use of general absolution in some situations may be the best or even the only way of satisfying this canonical duty.

Through no fault of their own. This means that the faithful have not deliberately created a situation in which it is impossible to have individual confessions in order that the confessor will have to resort to general absolution and they can avoid individual confession. This phrase again stresses the extraordinary nature of general absolution. Rite 3 cannot be licitly celebrated merely because people prefer it to individual confession.

Not just because of the great number of penitents. General absolution cannot be given only because there are many penitents and few confessors, as can happen, to use the example given in canon

961, "on the occasion of some great feast or pilgrimage." The code takes this example from the Rite of Penance, 31 to illustrate that all the conditions of the law must be met for using general absolution as detailed above, such as "rightly to hear," "within a suitable time," etc. The most important conditions are, nevertheless, the multitude of penitents and lack of readily available confessors.

Role of the Bishop

Canon 961, §2 grants competence to the diocesan bishop to judge whether the conditions required for general absolution are met. This does not mean that the diocesan bishop must always approve beforehand, or even afterwards, the use of general absolution in each particular case. Indeed, this is one area where the new code has broadened the former law on general absolution. The 1974 liturgical law stated:

> If, apart from the instances established by the local Ordinary, any other serious need arises for giving general absolution, a priest is bound first, whenever possible, to have recourse to the local Ordinary in order to give the general absolution. If this is not possible, he is to inform the same Ordinary as soon as possible of the need in question and of the fact of the absolution.[9]

This quoted paragraph was eliminated in the 1983 revision of the liturgical books following the promulgation of the revised Code of Canon Law. This change in law was not intended to prevent confessors from acting in cases of necessity not foreseen by the bishop. On the contrary, the pontifical commission that revised the code recognized that confessors can use general absolution in cases of serious necessity in virtue of "principles of moral theology," but they noted that the law is not the proper place to include such principles.[10] Among the principles of moral theology relevant here are excusing causes, such as physical and moral impossibility to observe the law, and epikeia, by which a law is not observed in a particular case in order to uphold a greater good.[11] In view of these principles, the confessor may sometimes resort to general absolution even in cases of grave need not foreseen by the bishop.

In effect, the elimination of the above-quoted provision from the Rite of Penance broadens the previous law. Since the new code went into effect there is no longer any obligation to inform the local Ordinary after the use of general absolution in cases of serious necessity not covered by particular law. It suffices in such cases that the conditions of the universal law be observed as treated above.

The intent of paragraph two of canon 961 is to allow the diocesan bishop to establish the typical kinds of cases when general absolution can be used in the diocese in keeping with the criteria of the episcopal conference, if such exist. A good example of such criteria is contained in the law enacted by the episcopal conference of Canada and approved by the Holy See:

> There may indeed arise situations that require recourse to general absolution. Across the country, these situations can arise only when there is a great number of faithful attending a religious ceremony, far beyond the number who can be heard by available confessors, either because this was unforeseeable, or because rigorous winter weather conditions and great distances prevent the presence of confessors, or because the number of priests in a region or diocese does not allow them to respond adequately in their normal working hours to several sessions of confessions in local Christian communities. [12]

In light of criteria enacted by the episcopal conference, the diocesan bishop can establish cases for general absolution in his diocese. He also is competent to establish such cases when the episcopal conference has not enacted general criteria. Moreover, he may even establish cases for the use of general absolution that are not envisioned by the episcopal conference if he has serious reasons for doing so. [13] Thus, the bishop is the principal authority for regulating the use of general absolution in his diocese.

The general cases of necessity established by the diocesan bishop may justify or require the celebration of Rite 3 even though the serious need cannot be characterized as creating an emergency situation. [14] For example, a certain diocese permits general absolution in three cases when the conditions of the universal law are met: (1) in hospitals and nursing homes; (2) on a retreat when communal penance is an integral part of the retreat experience; and (3) when a celebration of Rite 2 has been scheduled and there are too many penitents to use this rite properly. Of course, all the conditions of the universal law must still be met even in the cases established by the bishop in particular law.

The general cases established in particular law should not be considered *taxative,* that is, as excluding all other cases. It is possible that situations other than those determined by the bishop may arise when it will be necessary to use general absolution lest the penitents are forced to be deprived of the grace of the sacrament or holy communion for a long time through no fault of their own. In cases of serious necessity not foreseen by the bishop, the confessor can avoid abuses by ensuring that all the conditions of the universal law are present before resorting to general absolution.

Neither the universal law nor the local bishop can foresee all possible situations, and therefore the confessor may need to use general absolution even in a case not expressly stated by particular law. Although the use of general absolution in this situation is not explicitly provided for in the law, it is implicit in virtue of other, more fundamental values. These values not only include the general principles of moral theology, referred to by the pontifical commission that revised the code, but also principles found in the Code of Canon Law itself, especially the protection of the faithful's right to receive the sacraments (canon 213) and the general principle, stated in canon 1752, that "the salvation of souls is always the supreme law of the church."

Planning Communal Penance

Although the reconciliation of serious sinners by means of general confession and absolution is considered extraordinary in the law, it is by no means wholly excluded as some restrictive interpretations of the law would suggest. On the other hand, there are some interpretations which are too liberal, which extend the meaning of the words beyond what is written in the legal text. All the conditions of the law must be present before general absolution can be used licitly. It is not lawful that general absolution be used for reasons other than danger of death or grave need, no matter how theologically and pastorally sound such motives may be. For example, it would not be lawful for a priest to plan and announce a service of general confession and absolution. Rite 3 is meant to be used only in a case of serious need, and one does not plan to create cases of necessity.

There is nothing contrary to the intent of the law, however, with scheduling Rite 2, the Rite for Reconciliation of Several Penitents with Individual Confession and Absolution, provided those in charge of the service prudently try to have sufficient confessors available, if this is possible. The liturgical and ecclesial values promoted by communal penance are so important that Rite 2 should not be neglected even if there is a doubt concerning the number of penitents who may be coming for the celebration. Unlike the first rite of individual penance, the communal celebration of the sacrament is manifestly faithful to a fundamental principle of the liturgical reform that was enunciated in the Constitution on the Sacred Liturgy of Vatican II:

> Whenever rites, according to their specific nature, make provision for communal celebration involving the presence and active participation of the faithful, it is to be stressed that this way of celebrating them is to be preferred, as far as possible, to a celebration that is individual and, so to speak, private.[15]

Liturgical law, furthermore, implies that there is a value in communal penance not found in individual penance. "Communal celebration," states the Rite of Penance, "shows more clearly the ecclesial nature of penance."[16]

The universal law has no explicit restrictions against the use of Rite 2. Moreover, in light of the preference for communal celebration of sacraments expressed both in the law (canon 837) and at Vatican II (which is the principal source for the interpretation of contemporary church law), communal penance evidently is both legally and theologically the preferred manner of celebration. The pastoral implication is clear: Communal celebrations of the sacrament of penance using the second rite should not be neglected even if there is some doubt that too many penitents may arrive. The avoidance of Rite 2 not only would be legally unwarranted and liturgically unsatisfactory, it also would deprive the faithful from regularly celebrating communal penance, which they frequently find more meaningful than individual penance and thereby would deny them a liturgical celebration that disposes them better to receive the grace of the sacrament.

Obligations of the Penitent

An issue of doctrine is behind the restrictions of church law on the use of Rite 3. This doctrine, enunciated at the Council of Trent,[17] is contained in canon 960: "Individual and integral confession and absolution constitute the only ordinary way by which the faithful person who is aware of serious sin is reconciled with God and the church." Individual confession is the ordinary way that serious sins are remitted; general absolution is an extraordinary way. It is noteworthy that this teaching refers only to those conscious of serious sin, so there would not be a *doctrinal* problem with using general absolution for homogeneous groups, such as children or mentally handicapped persons, who are not conscious of being in serious sin. The canonical norms, however, do not make this distinction.

Proper disposition. Canon 962, §1 states: "For a member of the faithful validly to enjoy sacramental absolution given to many at one time, it is required that this person not only be suitably disposed but also at the same time intend to confess individually in due time the serious sins which at present cannot be so confessed." The proper disposition is necessary for the valid reception of the sacrament. This disposition includes contrition, or sorrow for the sins committed; the intention not to commit them again; and the intention to make reparation for scandal or harm that may have been caused. Another requirement related to proper disposition is contained in canon 969, §2, directed to the confessor: " . . . an exhortation that each person take care to make an act of contrition is to precede general absolution, even in danger of death if time is available."

Intention to confess serious sins. Canon 962, §1 requires more than proper disposition. It also obliges, for validity, that those receiving general absolution intend to confess individually at a later time their serious sins that cannot be so confessed presently. This law is most problematic. It is difficult for people to understand why sins must be confessed once they have already been absolved. Certainly one can assert that serious sinners often need individual attention and assistance in order for the continuing process of reconciliation to be more fruitful. But why should this be necessary for the validity of the general absolution? How is one to understand, theologically, that sins already forgiven constitute valid matter for confession? How does the confessor explain that after receiving sacramental absolution in one celebration, all those present who are in serious sin must return to a second celebration for the absolution of the same sins?

Rather than trying to give a rationale for this curious obligation at the time of a celebration of general absolution, it may be preferable simply to state what the law requires without adding pastoral or doctrinal explanations that likely would only confuse the penitents. This would fulfill the confessor's obligation given in canon 962, §2 which says: *As much as can be done,* the faithful are to be instructed concerning the requirements for valid general absolution (namely, that they be suitably disposed and intend to confess serious sins individually at a later time). The satisfaction of these obligations can then be left to the penitent's conscience and God's mercy.

Confession of serious sins. Another requirement of the faithful who receive general absolution is that of canon 963: "With due regard for the obligation mentioned in canon 989, a person who has had serious sins remitted by a general absolution is to approach individual confession as soon as there is an opportunity to do so before receiving another general absolution unless a just cause intervenes." Canon 989 is the precept to confess serious sins annually. This precept must be observed by all who have reached the age of discretion—not only those receiving general absolution—unless it is physically or morally impossible to do so. The reference to the precept in this context suggests that those who receive a general absolution must confess their serious sins individually even before the lapse of a year's time, unless a just cause intervenes.

As soon as there is opportunity. This refers to the time when the person in serious sin who has received a general absolution must confess individually and integrally the serious sin or sins. The time should be understood ordinarily as the next scheduled opportunity for individual penance that the person is able to attend or another opportunity that can be arranged without undue inconvenience to the confessor or penitent.

A just cause. The requirement of confessing individually one's serious sins after a general absolution as soon as there is opportunity does not bind when a just cause intervenes. Some examples of just causes would include: serious inconvenience to the penitent or the confessor; a remote area where sufficient priests are unavailable to guarantee a penitent needed anonymity or freedom of choice of confessors; a person who has an extreme fear of or aversion to individual confession.

Canon 963 is disciplinary, not doctrinal, in nature. A person who, without just cause, receives a second general absolution before individually confessing his or her unconfessed serious sins from a previous general absolution would act illicitly. However, the second absolution would be valid provided the person was properly disposed and intended to confess individually the serious sins in due time.

Conclusion

Those who know the history of the sacrament are well aware that penance has at times undergone significant changes in its ritual structure and pastoral practice. The emphasis of the contemporary liturgical reform on the communal celebration of all rites has likely created a new and significant shift in the ongoing evolution of this sacrament. This shift from an individual-centered discipline to one that recognizes the social and ecclesial dimensions of sin and reconciliation has led to tensions between persons in the church who have divergent viewpoints. These tensions are also reflected in official church documents, with some documents (such as the liturgy constitution of Vatican II and the Rite of Penance) lauding communal celebration, while others (such as the Code of Canon Law) ostensibly preferring the pre-Vatican II pattern of individual confession.

In light of these opposing emphases and the tension they produce, it is important to understand the meaning of the law in both text and context. This knowledge is necessary not only to protect the legitimate doctrinal considerations enshrined in the law, but also to prevent arbitrary and restrictive interpretations of the law that may unjustly deprive the faithful of their right to the grace of the sacrament through a meaningful liturgical celebration.

Notes

[1] *Reconciliatio et Paenitentia,* 33, December 2, 1984, AAS 77 (1985) 185-275. Translation in *Origins* 14 (1984) 453. For a study which helps to situate this document—as well as the provisions of the code on general absolution—in broader historical and theological context, see James Dallen, "Recent Documents on Penance and Reconciliation," in *Reconciliation: The Continuing Agenda,* ed. Robert J. Kennedy (Collegeville: Liturgical Press, 1987) 95-113. See also Ladislas Orsy, "General Absolution: New Law, Old Traditions, Some Questions," *Theological Studies* 45 (1984) 676-89; and *The Evolving Church and the Sacrament of Penance* (Denville, NJ: Dimension Books, 1978), especially 173-89.

[2] See, e.g., German Episcopal Conference, Erklärung, September 18, 1972, *Archiv für katholisches Kirchenrecht* 141 (1972) 522-23; Italian Episcopal Conference, Notificazione della Presidenza, March 22, 1974, *Enchiridion della Conferenza Episcopale Italiana* 2 (Bologna: 1985), n. 1171.

[3] Address, April 20, 1978, AAS 70 (1978) 328-32; DOL, 3138-39.

[4] Congregation for the Doctrine of the Faith, letter, January 14, 1977, DOL, 3127-32; Paul VI, address, April 3, 1974, *Notitiae* 10 (1974) 225-27; DOL, 3110-13.

[5] See Rite of Penance, 21.

[6] In announcing the initial vote on the resolution, Archbishop John May, the president of the NCCB, stated: "Its purpose is not to put an end to the practice of general absolution but to achieve insofar as possible a degree of common understanding and practice which in the long run will enhance the administration of the church's sacramental life." See *Origins* 18 (1988) 120. At the time of this writing the Holy See has not yet confirmed the NCCB decree.

[7] See Frederick R. McManus, CLSA Comm 679; H. Wagnon, "Les 'Normes pastorales' pour l'administration de l'absolution sacramentelle générale," *Revue Théologique de Louvain* 4 (1973) 55; Marcelino Zalba, "Commentarium ad normas pastorales circa absolutionem sacramentalem generali modo impertiendam," *Periodica* 62 (1973) 201. On the other hand, Jan Visser understands *diu* as a month or at least for some weeks; see "Le recenti norme circa l'assoluzione comunitaria," *Seminarium* 25 (1973) 582.

[8] For a different opinion see International Theological Commission, report, "Penance and Reconciliation," *Origins* 13 (1984) 522.

[9] Rite of Penance, 32; DOL, 3097.

[10]See the response of the Pontifical Commission for the Revision of the Code of Canon Law, *Communicationes* 15 (1983) 206.

[11]See Lawrence J. Riley, *The History, Nature and Use of Epikeia in Moral Theology* (Washington, DC: Catholic University of America, 1948); Frederick R. McManus, "Liturgical Law and Difficult Cases," *Worship* 48 (1974) 347-66; John Huels, *The Pastoral Companion* (Chicago: Franciscan Herald, 1986) 13-17.

[12]Criteria for General Absolution Established by the CCCB (Canadian Conference of Catholic Bishops), document n. 589, March 22, 1988.

[13]See Julio Manzanares, "De absolutione sacramentali generali in casu gravis necessitatis considerationes," *Periodica* 76 (1987) 143-144.

[14]See McManus, CLSA Comm 679.

[15]SC, 27; DOL, 27. See also canon 837.

[16]Rite of Penance, 22; DOL, 3087.

[17]Session XIV, *de paenitentia,* canon 7; DS 917.

Who May Be Anointed

The rite of the anointing of the sick[1] is surely among the most successful of the liturgical reforms following the Second Vatican Council. The rite was thoroughly revised to bring out more clearly its original purpose as a sacrament for the sick and not only the dying.

Since the Middle Ages pastoral practice had relegated this "last anointing" *(extrema unctio)* to the final moments before death. There was a strongly felt desire among the faithful that the priest be present to anoint dying persons, not in order that they might recover, but to remit any remaining sins they might have before their souls departed from this world for the next. In the 16th century, the Council of Trent taught that the sacrament both forgives sins and relieves the sick,[2] but until recently it continued to be associated by and large with the moment of death. The 1917 Code of Canon Law said that the sacrament could be administered to someone "in danger of death" (canon 940). Although not intended to restrict the anointing to those in "imminent" danger of death, that is how the law was generally observed.

Given this centuries-long praxis, it is indeed surprising that the reform of the sacrament has been so widely accepted. The new rite urges that the faithful be taught not to follow "the wrongful practice of delaying the reception of the sacrament" (PCS, 13). This catechesis has been successful. No longer is the anointing widely associated strictly with the dying. Unfortunately, an awareness of viaticum as the true "last rite" does not yet appear to be strongly rooted in piety or pastoral practice.

While some people still wait too long to request the sacrament, it seems that the greater abuse in recent years has been the practice of indiscriminate anointing, and this is especially a problem at communal services. In one parish a monthly communal anointing service is held and the priest invites all present to come forward for the anointing. In another parish the priest at a communal service announced that all persons 65 and over were welcome to request the anointing. One healthy young woman once stated at a workshop that she always receives the anointing at communal celebrations because she believes that "everyone is in need of inner healing." Although such blatant abuses may be few, there appears to be widespread confusion about who is truly eligible to be a recipient of the anointing.

Serious Illness

According to the church's law in both the Code of Canon Law and in Pastoral Care of the Sick, the sacrament may be administered only to those who are *seriously* ill, specifically those who begin to be in danger due to sickness or old age (canons 998; 1004, §1; PCS, 8). This includes those about to undergo surgery when a serious illness is the reason for the surgery (PCS, 10). The Latin uses the term *periculose,* rendered "seriously" in the English translation of the ritual in order to make it clear that the anointing is not only intended for those in danger of death. (This translation has been approved by the Apostolic See.)

The appropriate time to request the anointing is when seriously ill people begin to be in danger, that is, at the onset of a serious illness. They can be anointed again if they fall into a more serious crisis during the same illness or if, after recovery, they develop a serious illness again (canon 1004, §2). In keeping with the intent of the law, the anointing of the sick is most appropriately celebrated at moments of crisis in an illness, particularly at the onset of the illness. Pastoral ministers and those who are close to the sick are canonically obliged to see that seriously ill persons are supported by the sacrament at this time (canon 1001).

The law does not specify what constitutes a serious illness but leaves this determination to those involved, especially the priest who is minister of the sacrament: "A prudent or reasonably sure judgment, without scruple, is sufficient for deciding on the seriousness of an illness; if necessary a doctor may be consulted" (PCS, 8). In doubt whether the person is seriously ill, the minister may anoint (canon 1005).

The illness can be from any cause, such as a wound, disease, poisoning, bodily deterioration, etc. However, the anointing cannot be given to those who are in danger of death but who are not seriously ill; for example, a prisoner about to be executed or a soldier going into battle. Because a principal aspect of the rite is prayer for recovery from illness, the anointing should not be given to healthy people who are about to die from an extrinsic source. In these cases reconciliation and eucharist are the appropriate sacramental ministrations.

The law also says that *elderly people* can be anointed if they have become *notably weakened* even though no serious illness is present (PCS, 11). Not all elderly persons are eligible to be anointed. Many are in good health and do not consider themselves sick or feeble. It would be canonically illicit, and possibly insulting to elderly persons, to suggest that all of them should be anointed after a certain age.

The anointing can also be administered to those who have a *serious mental illness* and who can be comforted by the sacrament (PCS, 53). Many psychological illnesses are indeed serious, especially those classified as psychoses. However, the minister should exercise caution before anointing persons with serious mental illnesses. Such cases should always be handled on an individual basis in consultation with the person's physician.

Alcoholism

As the concept of alcoholism as a disease has gained prominence, the question at times arises whether alcoholics can be anointed. In this view, alcoholism is a debilitating and, at times, a terminal disease; therefore it is indeed a serious illness whose victims are eligible to receive the sacrament. Furthermore, since in this theory alcoholics are never fully cured even after they have ceased drinking, the sacrament of anointing can be beneficial in helping them to maintain sobriety.

While this position has some merit, it is not wholly convincing. Alcoholism is a unique kind of disease, symptoms of which disappear once the alcoholic completely stops drinking. Although alcoholics may be said to have the disease all their life even after they no longer drink, their illness ceases to be acute or manifest. Indeed, recovered alcoholics are not uncommonly heard to assert that they have "never felt better."

The sacrament of anointing is intended for those with a serious illness, especially in a crisis situation such as at the onset of the illness or before surgery. This is not the condition of alcoholics who have stopped drinking. They can more fittingly be strengthened spiritually by the sacraments of reconciliation and eucharist than by the anointing. On the other hand, in an acute phase of treatment when the alcoholic is suffering greatly, it is possible that, on a case-by-case basis, a determination could be made by the minister that the sacrament would be appropriate and beneficial.

Use of Reason

Those to be anointed must also have attained the use of reason (canon 1004). In doubt whether the person has attained the use of reason, the sacrament should be administered (canon 1005). The law presumes the use of reason is attained by age seven, but some children may have sufficient use of reason to receive the sacrament at a younger age. The ritual says that *children* can be anointed if they have sufficient use of reason to be strengthened *(confortari)* by the sacrament (PCS, 12). Even children under seven can be strengthened or comforted by the sacrament, especially when it is celebrated in the presence of family or others who care for them.

By analogy with this law, one could also say that *developmentally disabled* persons who lack the full use of reason, such as the mentally retarded, can be anointed if they can be comforted by the sacrament. They do not need to have an intellectual understanding of the sacrament or the ability to express their faith rationally; they only need the capacity to be strengthened by the celebration. It is important to remember, however, that mental retardation and other developmental disabilities are not illnesses but are permanent conditions of persons. They too must have a serious illness to be anointed.

The provision of Pastoral Care of the Sick, 53, allowing those with serious mental illnesses to be anointed if "they would be comforted by the sacrament" also is based on an analogy with the universal law governing the reception of anointing by young children. Although such persons may lack sufficient use of reason for many acts and may be incapable of certain sacraments, such as marriage or reconciliation, they may have sufficient use of reason to be comforted by the anointing.

It should be noted that the requirement of the use of reason applies only to those who have always lacked the use of reason. Baptized persons who once had the use of reason but subsequently lost their mental faculties due to senility, unconsciousness, mental illness or some other reason may nevertheless be anointed (canon 1006). According to the ritual, "The sacrament of anointing may be conferred upon sick people who, although they have lost consciousness or the use of reason, would, as Christian believers, probably have asked for it were they in control of their faculties" (PCS, 14).

Other Requirements

Those who wish to receive the anointing of the sick must meet several other canonical requirements. The most basic requirement for the valid reception of any sacrament is that the recipient be *baptized*. Moreover, in ordinary circumstances the anointing of the sick, as well as penance and eucharist, are licitly administered only to *Catholics*.

Catholic ministers may anoint separated Eastern Christians and those in canonically equivalent churches whenever such Christians ask for the sacrament on their own and are properly disposed. Protestants can be anointed in danger of death or for some other grave necessity when, in the judgment of the diocesan bishop or the conference of bishops, they cannot approach a minister of their own denomination, provided they ask for the sacrament on their own, manifest a Catholic faith in it and are properly disposed (canon 844).

As with all the sacraments, the anointing can be conferred only on *those who are alive*. When a priest is called to minister in a situation where a person has just died, it is fitting to use the prayers for the dead found in Pastoral Care of the Sick. If there is a genuine doubt whether the person is dead, the anointing can be administered (canon 1005).

The anointing is not to be conferred on *those who obstinately persist in manifest serious sin* (canon 1007). An example would be a person who has been excommunicated or interdicted and refuses reconciliation or one who has completely abandoned the practice of the faith and does not wish to return to the church. If such persons are unconscious, they cannot be anointed unless they had previously given some sign of repentance, for example, if before losing consciousness they had asked that a priest be summoned.

Communal Services

Parishes, hospitals and other institutions that have held communal anointing services have found them to be moving and effective in many respects, not only in the beauty of the liturgical rites and the spiritual comfort experienced by sick persons, but also in the growth of concern and charity for the sick on the part of those who are well. In many places such communal services have become a regular practice, held annually or more frequently.

Canon 1002 of the 1983 code permits communal celebrations of the anointing of the sick for many of the sick at the same time who are duly prepared and rightly disposed. It is important that the preparation for communal services also include clear instructions to the community on who is eligible to receive the sacrament. Parish staffs, liturgy teams and pastoral care departments in hospitals often need to make a special effort not only to provide such catechesis, but also to examine their own attitudes toward what constitutes a successful liturgical celebration.

A tendency of people in Western culture is to judge their own worth in terms of external success and they judge success is terms of output or popularity. In the context of communal anointing, the success mentality—the belief that more is better—can be a factor that contributes to an underemphasis or neglect of the canonical requirements. To ensure a large assembly and "successful" celebration, the organizers of communal celebrations might unwittingly be encouraging people to receive the anointing who are not eligible for it.

A problem especially in American society is the democratization of liturgy, the blurring of proper roles and ministries and the conscious or unconscious belief that since all people are created equal, all have the right to receive the sacraments. In connection with the sacrament of the sick, this misguided egalitarianism is patently absurd. It is like saying that all people, even those who are well or only mildly sick, have the right to major surgery, insurance payments or a sick leave from work.

More is at stake here than the observance of canon law. When healthy or slightly ill persons routinely receive the anointing, its symbolic value as a special sacrament reserved for the seriously ill is jeopardized. As liturgical theologian, Jennifer Glen, puts it: "Rites that attempt to include every meaning risk losing all meaning."[3]

Perhaps an analogy may help to clarify this point. If an important event, such as Christmas, were to be celebrated every day of the year, the unique sentiments attached to the feast would soon be lost and it would quickly become tiresome. So also, if the anointing of the sick is routinely given to those who are not eligible, its unique value as a sign of the church's special concern for its seriously ill members will also be lost.

Anointing is reserved for critical moments at the onset and during the progression of a serious illness or a notable weakening in the condition of an old person. At other times seriously ill persons, as well as other sick and elderly persons who are unable to participate in the eucharistic assembly, should seek more frequent spiritual nourishment through the sacrament of holy communion brought to them by ministers of pastoral care.[4]

Notes

[1]This and other rites and prayers for the sick and dying constitute the ritual book, *Pastoral Care of the Sick: Rites of Anointing and Viaticum* (PCS), which is the English text approved and mandated for use in the United States since 1983. Most of the numbered citations used in this essay from this version are the same as those found in the typical edition, the *Ordo unctionis infirmorum eorumque pastoralis curae* (Typis Polyglottis Vaticanis, 1975). For a good bibliography on the sacrament of the anointing of the sick and ministry to the sick, see Charles W. Gusmer, *And You Visited Me: Sacramental Ministry to the Sick and Dying* (New York: Pueblo, 1984) 203-11.

[2]Session XIV, 1551, D. de paenit. et unct. extr., cap. 2, DS 1696; canon 2, DS 1717.

[3]"Rites of Healing: A Reflection in Pastoral Theology," in *Alternative Futures for Worship,* volume 7: *Anointing of the Sick,* volume editor, Peter E. Fink (Collegeville: Liturgical Press, 1987) 60.

[4]Pastoral Care of the Sick, 72-73 emphasizes this point: "Priests with pastoral responsibilities should see to it that the sick or aged, even though not seriously ill or in danger of death, are given every opportunity to receive the eucharist frequently, even daily, especially during the Easter season. . . . In bringing communion to them the minister of communion represents Christ and manifests faith and charity on behalf of the whole community toward those who cannot be present at the eucharist. For the sick the reception of communion is not only a privilege but also a sign of support and concern shown by the Christian community for its members who are ill."

Mixed Marriages and Eucharist

The cause of ecumenism was greatly advanced by the Second Vatican Council which brought about a new, positive stance of the Catholic church toward other Christian denominations. This led to substantial changes in the church's discipline on interfaith matters. Among these have been changes in canon law governing mixed marriage. A mixed marriage, in the strict sense of the term and as used here, is a marriage between a Catholic and a *baptized* non-Catholic.

In the former law, liturgical ceremonies of any kind were prohibited at a mixed marriage without the Ordinary's permission and the celebration of the eucharist was always excluded.[1] With Pope Paul VI's 1970 *motu proprio, Matrimonia mixta,* marriages between a Catholic and a baptized non-Catholic could be celebrated at the eucharist with permission of the local Ordinary. They also could take place in the church of the non-Catholic party with the necessary dispensation from the law of the canonical form requiring the presence of a designated Catholic priest or deacon and two other witnesses.[2] A marriage between a Catholic and a nonbaptized party, even a catechumen, may not be celebrated at the eucharist.

The Ideal Situation

In places such as the United States, where there are many mixed marriages, it has become commonplace since 1970 to celebrate them at the eucharist. Ideally, the marriage of two Christians should have an explicit eucharistic context. Liturgical theologian M. Francis Mannion makes several points in this regard:

1. Since the eucharist is the primary expression of the church, it is the place where the salvific meaning of every ecclesial reality is established and celebrated. Thus it is the eucharistic context that reveals and illuminates the most profound dimensions of Christian marriage.

2. In the eucharist the particularity of each marriage is placed within the great acts of God in history and the particular nuptial union becomes, in a certain way, an invocation of the final union of the kingdom to come.

3. In the sharing of the broken bread and the common cup, the couple becomes one body in a mystery of unity that has no fuller expression than that set forth in the sacrament of the Lord's body.

4. Christian marriage, like all sacraments, is an Easter sacrament, a sacrament of the covenant love of God declared through Christ's paschal sacrifice. In essence, then, Christian marriage is agapic, sacrificial, eucharistic love and must be interpreted through the mystery of the cross.[3]

Doubtless, these theological values can find true expression in the eucharistic liturgy of marriage between two believing and practicing Catholics. In a mixed marriage, however, possibly divergent beliefs and practices, together with certain provisions of canon law, prevent this ideal situation from being readily attained.

Theological and Canonical Issues

From Martin Luther's day, Protestants by and large have not considered marriage to be a sacrament instituted by Christ. Accordingly, if the priest presides at the eucharist at a wedding between a Catholic and a Protestant in order to bring out the sacramentality of marriage, it may result in offending the beliefs of the Protestants present.

Regarding the doctrine of the eucharist, it seems highly unlikely that historically divisive issues—such as real presence, transubstantiation, the sacrificial character of the Mass—are truly troubling to many lay non-Catholic Christians attending a nuptial eucharist. But some may not truly feel "at home" at a wedding Mass. Perhaps they come from a largely word-centered tradition. Or even if they are accustomed to celebrating the Lord's supper, many of the Catholic prayers, responses, gestures and postures may be strange to them. Moreover, some of the guests, or even the bride and groom themselves, may not be practicing their faith and may not find the eucharist an especially meaningful addition to a church wedding. In any case, non-Catholics are not accustomed to celebrate eucharist at weddings.

With the increasing shortage of priests, there are also practical and canonical considerations that militate against the frequent celebration of the eucharist when it is unnecessary. Canon law does not allow local Ordinaries to permit priests to preside at or concelebrate more than two Masses on weekdays, including Saturdays, or more than three Masses on Sundays and holy days of obligation (canon 905, §2). In many places parish priests welcome the assistance of deacons to preside at the nuptial liturgy. Certain countries that have a severe shortage of priests rely on delegated lay persons to be the church's official witness of marriage, in accord with canon 1112. Since the shortage of priests seems certain to worsen, one can expect that celebrations of the eucharist, even at marriages between two Catholics, will become less common in the future than they are at present.

Sacramental Sharing

An even greater source of difficulty with the celebration of the eucharist at mixed marriages is the canon law restricting the reception of holy communion by non-Catholics. The discipline in question is based on the official position of the church that sacramental sharing *(communicatio in sacris)* is, in general, to be considered the goal of, not the means to, the unity of churches. Since the eucharist is a sign of the unity of the church, open communion (or intercommunion), according to the official Catholic viewpoint, is not possible until such unity is actually achieved. Since the sacraments are also sources of grace, however, canon law permits baptized non-Catholics in particular cases, under specified conditions, to receive communion (and also penance and anointing of the sick).

The liturgical law in the 1969 Rite of Marriage adverts to the general policy of the church on intercommunion in reference to mixed marriages: "If the situation warrants and if the local Ordinary gives permission, the rite for celebrating marriage within Mass may be used [at mixed marriages], except that communion is not given to the non-Catholic, since the general law does not allow it."[4] This does not mean that communion can never be given to the non-Catholic party. Rather, it refers to the *lex generalis*—other relevant sources of universal law including that of Vatican II and the Ecumenical Directory.[5] This discipline allows communion to be given to Eastern Christians who do not have full communion with the Catholic church and to members of other churches, which in the judgment of the Apostolic See are in the same condition as the oriental churches as far as these sacraments are concerned, provided they ask for the sacrament on their own and are properly disposed (canon 844, §3). The law also allows holy communion to be given to other Christians (Protestants) who do not have full communion with the Catholic church but who meet the several conditions of canon 844, §4, given below.

The Catholic church is quite open to the possibility of sacramental sharing with Eastern Christians and others belonging to churches that have a valid priesthood, true sacraments and apostolic succession.[6] Thus, there is no doctrinal or canonical problem with celebrating and administering the eucharist at a wedding between a Catholic and an Eastern Christian, at least not from the Catholic standpoint. Very often, however, Eastern Christians are prohibited by their own church from receiving the eucharist in other churches. If the Eastern party does not wish to receive holy communion, it may be preferable not to have a wedding Mass lest it appear that the non-Catholic is being denied the eucharist or lacks the proper disposition.

Protestants do not enjoy as favorable a position in canon law as the Eastern churches. The Ecumenical Directory and canon 844, §4 of the Code of Canon Law contain quite restrictive provisions for sacramental sharing with Protestants. For a Protestant to receive communion from a Catholic minister the following conditions must be verified: (1) it is a case of danger of death or another serious necessity in the judgment of the diocesan bishop or the conference of bishops; (2) the person cannot approach a minister of his or her own church and receive communion; and (3) the person manifests Catholic faith in the eucharist and has the proper disposition.

There may be times when a Protestant party to a mixed marriage fulfills these conditions,[7] and various dioceses have policies which acknowledge this possibility. However, even in a case where permission is granted to administer communion to a Protestant party in a mixed marriage, it would not be lawful to offer holy communion to the other Protestant guests because it would be virtually impossible to verify the conditions of canon law for a whole group attending a wedding.

Thus, even if the Protestant party to the marriage receives permission from the bishop to receive communion, the Protestant guests who are present could not lawfully be invited to approach the Lord's table. As a result, a notable problem arises on the level of symbol. When two Christians marry, the assembly gathers to celebrate a sacramental union. When a significant part of that community is excluded from the Lord's supper, however, the sign conveyed is that of division rather than unity. The celebration of the eucharist in such a situation might tend to diminish the goodwill of non-Catholics toward the Catholic church rather than truly promote the cause of Christian unity.

From time to time one hears reports of individual priests who take the law into their own hands and invite all present at a mixed-marriage liturgy to come to communion. Although such priests presumably have good intentions, their action in violation of the church's law often causes more harm than good. It is widely known that the Catholic church does not permit open communion. Such an invitation on the part of a priest acting on his own authority can cause bewilderment in both Catholics and non-Catholics who are present. Even those in the assembly who are not disturbed by the breaking of the law might not want to go to communion for their own reasons, perhaps because they are not properly disposed, or perhaps because they are prohibited by their own church from taking communion in other churches. Announcing at a wedding that "everybody is welcome to come to communion" calls attention to people who do not participate and may cause them embarrassment.

How to Decide

For all the reasons given above, especially the canonical restrictions on sacramental sharing and the disunity signified when part of the assembly is unable to fully participate, it is better, as a rule, not to celebrate the eucharist at a mixed marriage involving a Catholic and a Protestant. The determination of whether the eucharist is to be celebrated should be made by the priest (or other minister or catechist) and the engaged parties in the course of the couple's preparation for the marriage. In making this decision, the priest should recognize that the Catholic party who requests the eucharist for the wedding often does so for reasons which are not altogether clearly understood and which may have little to do with his or her own personal devotion or the value placed on the sacraments of eucharist and marriage. It is useful for the priest to uncover in a discreet manner the motivation for desiring the eucharist. Is it simply to have greater solemnity and a longer ceremony? Is it only to please the Catholic parents and relatives? Have the views and preferences of the non-Catholic party and guests been considered?

Non-Catholics may have misgivings about having their wedding during the eucharist. Often they do not express these misgivings for fear of offending the Catholic minister or because they do not want to disturb the Catholic party who wants to have a wedding Mass. The Protestant participants and guests at a wedding frequently feel more comfortable with the liturgy of the word than the Catholic Mass.

The Catholic party who wants a wedding Mass often is not aware that it is possible to have a beautiful and meaningful wedding with procession, music and song, scripture readings, acclamations, homily, intercessions, blessings and all the principal symbols and rites of the marriage liturgy. These ritual elements are also common to most Protestant liturgies, including their wedding liturgies.

Ecumenical sensitivity requires respect for the doctrinal as well as liturgical traditions of other Christian faiths. Above all, the presider at a Catholic/Protestant wedding ought to avoid overt references to the sacramentality of marriage (in the narrow sense of "sacrament" as one of the seven). Rather, he could speak of the covenant of marriage and stress values intrinsic to the sacrament that are shared with other Christians, such as fidelity, commitment, perpetuity, family and a marriage in church in the presence of God and community.

Communion Only during Mass

A word might also be added about the practice of distributing communion at wedding liturgies apart from Mass. The Rite of Marriage allows for this possibility when Mass cannot be celebrated as, for example, in areas where there is no local resident priest.[8] However, this practice is unnecessary in places where the Sunday eucharist is regularly celebrated and Catholics have sufficient opportunity to receive communion apart from the wedding ceremony without the Mass, whether a priest or deacon presides at it.

In accord with the teaching of Vatican II and the discipline of the revised Code of Canon Law, communion should be administered *during the eucharist* itself, except for a just reason.[9] When the parties to a marriage and the assembled faithful have the opportunity to attend Sunday eucharist, there ordinarily seems no need to neglect this important liturgical principle by offering communion at a wedding liturgy without Mass. If, for reasons of piety, the couple wants to receive communion on their wedding day and there is to be no Mass at their wedding liturgy, they can be encouraged to participate and receive communion in a regularly scheduled eucharist celebrated that day in their own parish or elsewhere.

Notes

[1] 1917 Code of Canon Law, canon 1102, §2.

[2] *Matrimonia mixta,* 9, 11, March 31, 1970, AAS 62 (1970) 257-63; DOL, 3007-08.

[3] "The Four Elements of Love," *Liturgy: Celebrating Marriage,* Journal of the Liturgical Conference 4 (Spring 1984) 20.

[4] Rite of Marriage, 8; DOL, 2976.

[5] Vatican II, Decree on Ecumenism, *Unitatis redintegratio,* 15, November 21, 1964, AAS 57 (1965) 90-107, DOL, 187; Vatican II, Decree on the Oriental Churches, *Orientalium Ecclesiarum,* 27, November 21, 1964, AAS 57 (1965) 76-85, DOL, 179; Secretariat for Christian Unity, Ecumenical Directory, Part I, *Ad totam Ecclesiam,* 38-45, May 14, 1967, AAS 59 (1967) 574-92, DOL, 992-99.

[6] Decree on Ecumenism, 15. For the sake of simplicity, the Eastern non-Catholic churches (e.g., the Orthodox) and their canonical equivalents referred to in canon 844, §3 will be identified in this essay as Eastern churches and their members as Eastern Christians.

[7] See, e.g., James Provost, "Canon 844," in *Roman Replies and CLSA Advisory Opinions* (Washington DC: CLSA, 1984) 43-46; and John Huels, "Select Questions of Eucharistic Discipline," in *Proceedings of the 47th Annual Convention of the CLSA* (Washington DC: CLSA, 1986) 48-53.

[8] See Rite of Marriage, 54. A case can also be made, from a liturgical viewpoint, for not holding communion services as a regular practice even in areas without a priest. See Gabe Huck, "Priestless Sundays: Are We Looking or Leaping?" *Liturgy 80* 18 (October 1987) 4-5.

[9] SC, 55; canon 918.

Concerts
in Churches

On November 5, 1987, the Vatican Congregation for Divine Worship issued a letter to the world's bishops on the use of churches for concerts of vocal or instrumental music.[1] Following its release, the Catholic press in the United States widely reported the document's allegedly restrictive provisions, including its negative stance on concerts of secular music in churches; its requirement of the Ordinary's permission to hold concerts in churches; and its prohibitions against charging admission, holding a series of concerts and positioning the performers in the sanctuary. Such reporting understandably occasioned great concern and dismay among church musicians and other interested persons. However, from a canonical perspective, there is no call for alarm. The congregation's letter does not really impose new restrictions on concerts held in churches. Indeed, when the document is read in its entirety and viewed in light of correct principles of canonical interpretation,[2] it can even be understood as a statement in support of concerts in churches.

Nature of the Document

To discover the letter's true intent, it is necessary to understand its nature and its relation to existing canonical norms. Whenever a document is issued by ecclesiastical authority, especially by the Apostolic See, the first questions that should be asked pertain to its nature, importance and binding force. There are dozens of kinds of documents issued by the pope and the Roman curia, and they have different degrees of doctrinal or juridic weight.

The document in question is a *letter written to bishops* from the Congregation for Divine Worship which intends to make "some observations and interpretations of the canonical norms concerning the use of churches for various kinds of music" (n. 3). It is not a legislative document. It does not purport to establish new canon law. The congregations of the Roman curia are executive, not legislative, bodies. To issue legislation they need express delegation from the pope who must review the document and order it to be published, but such is not the case with this document.

While the congregations of the Roman curia are not legislative, they can issue instructions or decrees that may contain binding administrative norms that are in accord with the law itself. However, the letter has no new binding norms at all, neither legislative nor administrative. Rather, the document serves to provide some helpful guidelines for bishops, Ordinaries, national and diocesan commissions for liturgy and music, and pastors and other rectors of churches who may want to make use of them in some way in order to establish local policies. Anything new in this document that is not already found in canon law is wholly optional.

Context of the Letter

The first section of the letter (nn. 1-4) sets the context. It speaks of the increased number of concerts held in churches in some countries and notes several advantages in favor of this practice. It says that "music and song contribute to elevating the human spirit," and that because of acoustical, aesthetical, practical and other reasons, churches are considered fitting places for holding a concert (n. 1). It recognizes the desirability of holding concerts of traditional sacred music in churches because such music frequently cannot be performed during the reformed liturgy (n. 2). Despite these and other positive reasons cited in support of concerts in churches, the congregation notes that their increased number "has given rise to doubts in the minds of pastors and rectors of churches as to the extent to which such events are really necessary" (n. 3).

Press reports have indicated that the Holy See is responding here to a dispute in Italy where some people have objected to the widespread use of churches for musical performances. The Vatican letter itself indicates that this dispute is indeed the pertinent context for the issuance of the letter, but it carefully avoids favoring one position over the other. It says that "a general opening of churches for concerts could give rise to complaints by a number of the faithful, yet on the other hand an outright refusal could lead to some misunderstanding" (n. 3). This balanced view sets the tone that the congregation attempts to maintain throughout the letter.

The final part of the introduction notes the importance of other pertinent documents and it mentions in particular the Constitution on the Sacred Liturgy of Vatican II, the 1967 instruction *Musicam sacram,* the 1970 instruction *Liturgicae instaurationes* and canons 1210, 1213 and 1222 of the Code of Canon Law.[3] This documentation not only serves as background for the letter, but it also establishes the parameters in which it should be interpreted.

Content of the Letter

After the introductory section there are two other sections entitled "Points for Consideration" (nn. 5-7) and "Practical Directives" (nn. 8-11). Section II begins by developing the theoretical basis for the practical directives that follow in the third section. The document stresses the point that churches are sacred places. They are set apart in a permanent way for divine worship by their dedication or blessing. The letter speaks of the symbolic value of churches as "the house of God and the sign of his dwelling among people." When churches are used for secular purposes, the document notes that their role as a sign may be jeopardized (n. 5).

Although the "primary concern" of the document is musical performances outside the liturgy (n. 4), the remainder of section II treats the role of music and the organ during the liturgy. A chief point made here is that "any performance of sacred music which takes place during a [liturgical] celebration should be fully in harmony with that celebration." Therefore, "this often means that musical compositions which date from a period when the active participation of the faithful was not emphasized as the source of the authentic Christian spirit . . . are no longer to be considered suitable for inclusion within liturgical celebrations" (n. 6).

Following this are several paragraphs devoted to the role of the organ in the liturgy. It may initially appear that the letter downplays the role of the organ except as a support to congregational singing, but a careful reading does not warrant this conclusion. The letter acknowledges that there is a place, albeit limited, for purely instrumental pieces on the organ during the liturgy. Nor does the letter prohibit the use of the organ during Lent and Holy Week, but states that it may be used when there is pastoral need (n. 7). In any case, none of the provisions on the organ should be understood as establishing new discipline but only as reinforcing what already is contained in earlier documents and legislation.

The third section, "Practical Directives," begins by citing canon 1210 of the Code of Canon Law, a canon with particular relevance to the principal concern of the letter. Canon 1210 states: "Only those things which serve the exercise or promotion of worship, piety or religion are to be admitted into a sacred place; anything which is not in accord with the holiness of the place is forbidden. The Ordinary, however, can permit other uses which are not contrary to the holiness of the place, in individual instances."[4]

Since this canon is the primary legal basis for the guidelines offered in the letter, it would be worthwhile to examine it closely. The canon speaks of "sacred places," which include not only churches but also oratories, private chapels, shrines, altars and cemeteries. Without the permission of the Ordinary, none of these sacred places are to be used for any purposes other than those which serve the exercise or promotion of worship, piety or religion. An Ordinary is a generic term which includes the diocesan bishop, vicar general, episcopal vicar and the major superior of a clerical religious institute or a clerical society of apostolic life.

The Vatican letter distinguishes between sacred music and religious music. Sacred music is composed for the liturgy, even if it can no longer be performed during the liturgy due to the liturgical reforms. Religious music is inspired by scripture or the liturgy and has reference to God, the Blessed Virgin Mary, the saints or the church. The determination of whether music is sacred, religious or secular is based on "the original intended use of the musical pieces or songs, and likewise on their content" (n. 8).[5] Both sacred and religious music, according to the document, are in accord with the sacred character of churches. The letter explicitly states that such music may "serve to promote piety or religion" and it lists six different ways that this is accomplished.[6]

Already in May 1987, in an address to the Congregation for Divine Worship, Pope John Paul II affirmed the value of concerts of religious music in churches without denying the value of secular music of good quality. He said that concerts of religious music outside of liturgical celebrations "can be an occasion offered to Christians who are no longer practicing their faith or even to non-Christians who are seeking God to have access to a true religious experience beyond a simple aesthetic emotion." He added: "In this manner the church will remain, even through artistic presentations with no liturgical connection, the place where one can discover the presence of the living God, the source of all beauty."[7] Clearly, both the pope and the Congregation for Divine Worship place a high value on concerts of religious music in churches.

Insofar as sacred and religious music "serves the promotion of piety or religion" in churches, in the words of canon 1210, it is not canonically necessary to secure the Ordinary's permission for a concert of such music to be held in a church.[8] The consent of the pastor or rector of the church would suffice. The judgment of the Ordinary would come into play when there is a dispute whether the sacred or religious music to be performed truly promotes piety or religion, or whether it truly is sacred or religious music. If, for example, a pastor objects to a concert on the grounds of the kind of music to be performed, the organizers of the concert could rightly make recourse to the Ordinary who, ideally acting on the advice of a musical commission or other experts, would determine whether the concert may take place.

The Ordinary's intervention is strictly necessary only in cases when the church is to be used for a purpose which does *not* serve the exercise or promotion of worship, piety or religion. In view of the congregation's letter, concerts of purely secular music are in this category. The letter states:

> It is not legitimate to provide for the execution in the church of music which is not of religious inspiration and which was composed with a view to performance in a certain precise secular context, irrespective of whether the music would be judged classical or contemporary, of high quality or of a popular nature. On the one hand such performances would not respect the sacred character of the church, and on the other would result in the music being performed in an unfitting context. (n. 8)

It is important to be aware of the fact that these quoted statements in no way canonically prohibit all concerts of secular music in churches. In keeping with the express purpose of this letter, they are "observations and interpretations" based on canon 1210 by the Congregation for Divine Worship. In the judgment of the congregation, secular music does not serve the promotion of piety or religion. It follows from this interpretation and from canon 1210 that the performance of a concert of purely secular music in a church would necessitate the Ordinary's permission. It also follows from canon 1210 that if the Ordinary judges that the quality and nature of the secular music to be performed is such that it would not be "contrary to the holiness of the place," he could permit such a concert in individual instances.

Specific Restrictions

It has already been noted that the Vatican letter does not make new law for the church. This must be kept in mind when reading the restrictive guidelines in the latter part of the letter. The first of these appear in the first paragraph of n. 10 which states that concerts in churches should be occasional events, excluding the possibility of a series of concerts. It appears that only concerts of secular music are intended to be so restricted. This paragraph of the letter evidently is based once again on canon 1210 which states that the Ordinary's permission is needed to use a sacred place for purposes other than those which serve the exercise or promotion of worship, piety or religion, and that this permission is granted *per modum actus*. This Latin phrase, which means "in individual instances," is used in both canon 1210 and the congregation's letter.

The letter must be understood in light of the law on which it is based. Since the Holy See acknowledges that sacred or religious music may indeed serve to promote piety or religion, a *series* of concerts of such music does not seem to be excluded. The concerts that should be restricted to occasional events requiring the permission of the Ordinary on a case-by-case basis are only concerts of *secular* music.

Of the eight specific guidelines which follow in n. 10 of the letter, it must again be stressed that, insofar as they are not based on already established canon law, they are wholly optional. According to the letter, the Ordinary "can specify" these guidelines, which means he can make normative in the churches in his jurisdiction one or several or all of them, but he is not obligated to impose them. Two examples may serve to illustrate this principle of interpretation.

One of the guidelines in the document that Ordinaries are free to implement has to do with the question of charging admission to concerts in churches. It states: "Entrance to the church must be without payment and open to all" (n. 10, c). This is not a requirement of canon law. Canon 1221 states: "Entrance to a church *during the time of sacred celebrations* is to be free and gratuitous." Universal church law does not exclude the possibility of selling tickets for a concert or requiring a donation of a fixed amount. However, an Ordinary may forbid this practice if he so chooses.

Another suggested guideline would prohibit the musicians and singers from performing in the sanctuary (n. 10, e). This, too, does not have the force of law. An Ordinary may make such an outright restriction if he desires, but it would be wiser for the pastor or rector of the church to determine the positioning of the performers on the basis of pastoral, aesthetical, acoustical and related concerns.

Conclusions

1. The November 5, 1987 letter of the Congregation for Divine Worship on concerts in churches is not a legislative document. It contains no new binding norms. Rather, it establishes background principles and suggests guidelines which may be helpful to those preparing local policies. The Ordinary is free to determine whether and to what extent the guidelines should be implemented for the churches in his jurisdiction.

2. Unless particular law (e.g., diocesan law) determines something else, concerts of sacred or religious music require only the permission of the pastor or other rector of the church. Universal law does not exclude a series of such concerts, nor does it prohibit the charging of admission for them.

3. The sponsorship of concerts of secular music in churches, in light of the interpretation of canon 1210 given in the congregation's letter, requires the permission of the Ordinary on a case-by-case basis. The Ordinary for diocesan churches is either the diocesan bishop, vicar general or episcopal vicar. The Ordinary for churches and oratories owned by a clerical religious institute or a clerical society of apostolic life is the major superior.

In light of this canonical analysis, it can hardly be maintained that the Holy See is opposed to using churches for musical performances. The contrary is true, especially when the concerts in question are of sacred or religious music. The congregation's letter ends quite positively, supporting the art of church music. It says, "The treasury of sacred music is a witness to the way in which Christian faith promotes culture." It encourages church musicians and choirs "to continue this tradition and to keep it alive for the service of the faith" (n. 11). When this letter is read in its entirety and correctly interpreted, it becomes clear that an important way in which this tradition is kept alive is by the continued sponsorship of concerts of high-quality music in Catholic churches.

Notes

[1] The letter, sent to the presidents of episcopal conferences and the presidents of national liturgical commissions, was first published in *L'Osservatore Romano,* December 6, 1987. It was published in English, French, German, Spanish and Italian in *Notitiae* 24 (January 1988). The English version, pp. 3-10, is used here with minor changes to provide for American spelling and inclusive language. A virtually identical English version also appeared in *Origins* 17 (1987) 468-70.

[2] On the interpretation of liturgical law, see John Huels, *Liturgical Law: An Introduction* (Washington DC: Pastoral Press, 1987); idem, *One Table, Many Laws* (Collegeville: Liturgical Press, 1986), chapter 1; and R. Kevin Seasoltz, *New Liturgy, New Laws* (Collegeville: Liturgical Press, 1980), chapters 13-15.

[3] See DOL, documents 1, 508 and 52.

[4] I have altered the CLSA translation slightly by using the word "or" instead of "and" in the phrase, "worship, piety *or* religion." The Latin original is open to either interpretation. It is contrary to experience and common sense to suggest that everything done in all sacred places must simultaneously serve the exercise or promotion of worship, piety "and" religion. A private visit to a Catholic cemetery, for example, may be an exercise in piety, but one would hardly call it an exercise of worship.

[5] Edward J. McKenna, a composer and musician, disputes the correctness of this distinction. See "It Can Do Damage in America," *Pastoral Music* 12 (April-May 1988) 35-36. This entire issue of *Pastoral Music* is devoted to responses to the congregation's letter from various viewpoints: liturgical, canonical, architectural and musical.

[6] The six ways that musical performances may serve to promote piety and religion are by: (a) preparing for the major liturgical feasts or lending to these a more festive character beyond the moment of actual celebration; (b) bringing out the particular character of the different liturgical seasons; (c) creating in churches a setting of beauty conducive to meditation, so as to arouse even in those who are distant from the church an openness to spiritual values; (d) creating a context which favors and makes accessible the proclamation of God's word; (e) keeping alive the treasures of church music which must not be lost, musical pieces and songs composed for the liturgy but which cannot in any way be conveniently incorporated into liturgical celebrations in modern times, and spiritual music such as oratorios and religious cantatas which can still serve as vehicles for spiritual communication; (f) assisting visitors and artists to grasp more fully the sacred character of a church by means of organ concerts at prearranged times.

[7]Address, May 22, 1987; translation in *Origins* 17 (1987) 128.

[8]This is also the view of Frederick R. McManus. See "How Legal Is It?" *Pastoral Music* 12 (April-May 1988) 23-26.

Acknowledgments

All translations of canons from the Code of Canon Law are taken from *Code of Canon Law: Latin-English Edition* copyright 1983 by Canon Law Society of America, used with permission. Excerpts from the English translation of *Documents on the Liturgy, 1963-1979: Conciliar, Papal and Curial Texts* (Collegeville: The Liturgical Press) © 1982, International Committee on English in the Liturgy, Inc. All rights reserved.

Chapters 1-6 and 8-11 are revisions of articles that originally were published as follows:

1. "The Age of Confirmation: A Canonist's View." *Catechumenate* 9 (November 1987) 30-36.
2. "Lay Preaching in Canon Law." *Emmanuel* 94 (1988) 244-51.
3. "Female Altar Servers: The Legal Issues." *Worship* 57 (1983) 513-25.
4. "Concelebration: Sign of Unity or Division?" *Liturgy 80* 18 (April 1987) 2-4.
5. "Stipend Intentions and the Eucharist." *Liturgy 80* 14 (October 1983) 4-6.
6. "Reducing the Number of Sunday Masses." *Emmanuel* 94 (1988), 376-81, 400-01.
8. "Canonical Perspectives on General Absolution." *Emmanuel* 93 (1987) 76-83, 90-91, 103.
9. "Who May Be Anointed?" *Liturgy 80* 19 (May-June 1988) 5-7.
10. "Should the Eucharist Be Celebrated at Mixed Marriages?" *Liturgy 80* 18 (January 1988) 12-15.
11. "Canonical Comments on Concerts in Churches." *Worship* 62 (1988) 165-72.

The author is grateful to the editor of *Worship* and to the editor of *Emmanuel* for permission to use material that originally appeared in these journals.

Index of Canons from the 1983 Code

Index of Laws from Liturgical Books